A SPLENDID GIFT

INDIGORIVER
PUBLISHING

A
SPLENDID
Celebrating Sixty
Years in Nursing
GIFT

A Memoir by

BARBARA ELLE PRISCEAUX

A Splendid Gift: Celebrating Sixty Years in Nursing

© 2023 by Barbara Elle Prisceaux

Library of Congress Control Number: 2023907791
ISBN: 978-1-954676-53-4 (print)   978-1-954676-54-1 (ebook)

Although this publication is designed to provide accurate information about the subject matter, the publisher and the author assume no responsibility for any errors, inaccuracies, omissions, or inconsistencies herein. This publication is intended as a resource, however, it is not intended as a replacement for direct and personalized professional services.

Editors: Deborah Froese, Mary Menke, David Remy
Cover and Interior Design: Emma Elzinga

Printed in the United States of America
First Edition

3 West Garden Street, Ste. 718
Pensacola, FL 32502

www.indigoriverpublishing.com

Ordering Information:
Quantity sales: Special discounts are available on quantity purchases by corporations, associations, and others. For details, contact the publisher at the address above.

Orders by US trade bookstores and wholesalers: Please contact the publisher at the address above.

With Indigo River Publishing, you can always expect great books, strong voices, and meaningful messages. Most importantly, you'll always find . . . *words worth reading.*

For my mother, Laura Allman Blanning,
and my sister, Carroll Blanning Linabury.

They loved books, encouraged me to write them,
and would have loved to read this one.

Live your life so that your children can tell their children that you not only stood for something wonderful—you acted on it.

Personal Mission Statement of Dan Zadra, Author

INTRODUCTION

HAPPINESS IS WRITING your own story.

When I was seventy-five, grateful for the incredible career that had continued longer than I'd ever thought possible, I finally started writing mine. Before I realized it, all those anecdotes about my adventures and misadventures in nursing took on a life of their own and became this book.

My nursing career began with a fall. Readers of *A Splendid Gift* will discover how I survived that near disaster and many more in a professional journey that lasted more than sixty years. Nursing led me from New York to Texas to Washington to California and, finally, to Florida. Too often to count, that career both challenged me and threatened to break my heart but also helped me make a real difference in the lives of my patients and their families.

A Splendid Gift is for anyone who is currently working in nursing, has ever worked in nursing, or is considering nursing as a primary or secondary career. It's also for anyone employed in the allied healthcare specialties or who has ever been the recipient of healthcare. Finally, it's for anyone interested in nursing history or curious about how increasing nursing expertise and evolving biomedical technology have changed the face of modern healthcare.

Florence Nightingale once wrote, "Live life if you have it. Life is a splendid gift."

My life in nursing continued far longer and had more twists and turns than I had ever thought possible. I'm grateful for all of them, and writing about those extraordinary years is something I have always been destined to do.

I hope you enjoy it.

Chapter One

A LAMP IS HEAVY

OH, NO! I'M doomed!

That's what I thought as I tripped at the top of the stairs at the Port Authority Bus Terminal and bounced off every one of them on the way to the subway platform below. Mortified to have fallen in the first place, the hopeful me wondered, *Will anyone stop and save me?*

Not likely! the cynical me answered as the crowd of fellow passengers on the platform parted like the Red Sea and skittered away from me in all directions. The practical me knew I had no option but to save myself. On my way to probably the most important interview of my life, there would be no second chances.

Grateful that nothing was broken, I muttered "Now or never," got up, and caught the next train downtown to Twenty-Third Street. From the way I looked, battered and bloody from the fall down the stairs, no taxi was about to stop for me. My stockings had shredded, and I'd lost the heel from one of my new, navy blue shoes. Blood stained the front of my skirt, and the left sleeve of the suit jacket hung by a thread. Tears streaked my face, and although I didn't dare look into a mirror, I suspected that the mascara I'd applied so carefully to my lashes that morning had already raccooned my eyes. Certain my morning was a complete disaster, I limped across town to First Avenue, back uptown to Twenty-Sixth Street, and arrived just in time for that long-anticipated interview at Bellevue Hospital Medical Center.

I'd always been in a hurry. Born one week early, on my sister Carroll's first birthday, I was a fragile four-pounder, not expected to survive. I spent my first six weeks in an incubator at Boston Lying-In Hospital, twiddling my tiny thumbs and waiting for my real life to begin. When I finally went home, my first crib was the bottom drawer in my parents' bedroom dresser.

By the time I was five and starting kindergarten, we'd moved from Massachusetts to New York to Florida and back to New York, and although nurses, doctors, hospitals, and patients would eventually become an obsession, I originally wanted to be a cowgirl or a ballerina. But more tomboy than girly-girl, cowboy boots beat out ballet slippers, and the freedom and fun of those tomboy years made me forget all about ballet.

My family lived in Yonkers at the top of Locust Hill Avenue, a twisting, turning city street perfect for sleds and toboggans in the winter and bicycles and roller skates in the summer. On my way back and forth to school between ages six and twelve and during the summers in between, I'd become fascinated by the comings and goings of all the nurses as they left their residence at the end of the block, on the way to classes or off to the hospital several streets away. I read and re-read all the books, including the *Sue Barton, Student Nurse* series and *A Lamp Is Heavy by Sheila MacKay Russell.* With no idea what nurses did when they went to work, I nevertheless wanted to be one. Florence Nightingale, The Lady with the Lamp who had revolutionized nursing and patient care, became my absolute hero, and I wanted to be just like her.

Intrepid tomboy turned awkward teenager, I was fourteen when I moved with my family to West Lawn, Pennsylvania, and began to focus on what I'd be doing for the rest of my life. Nursing again became a goal, and although I'd never been inside a hospital, at fifteen I decided to get a job at one.

Old enough to qualify for working papers, I applied for a position as a nurse's aide at St. Joseph's, the Sisters of Mercy Hospital in

Reading, twenty miles away. My hours were after school from 4 to 7 p.m. and from 10 a.m. to 7 p.m. on weekends whenever they needed me. That meant running for the bus on weekdays, a mile or so from Wilson High, and taking it into town on the weekends. In that two-hundred-bed hospital, dealing with medical professionals, young and older adults, children and their families, I overcame my paralyzing shyness. At sixteen, I witnessed my first death. At seventeen, I held a dying baby in my arms. That was real. That was where I was meant to be. Sister Marie Cecilia became my mentor and encouraged me to pursue my dreams. I owe that early sense of commitment and purpose to her.

By then, I'd begun sending for literature from nursing schools across the country.

"But why go so far away?" my mother asked when I told her I was considering Massachusetts General in Boston, Cook County in Chicago, and County General in Los Angeles.

"Because any of them will provide the education and experience I'll need, but I want adventures too," I admitted.

"You had those. You left Tennessee when you were eighteen, went all the way out to California on your own, and worked there until you were twenty."

She laughed with me about the adventures and agreed I should have them, but a book I received for my birthday that year changed everything. Jack Engeman's *Student Nurse*, a photographic tribute to New York City's famous Bellevue Hospital Center and School of Nursing, became my most treasured resource. I'd already read and reread *Bellevue Is My Home* by hospital administrator Salvatore Cutolo, MD. I knew that the nursing school had been founded in the 1870s based on precepts set by Florence Nightingale. Growing up in Westchester County, New York, I'd often heard of the famous Bellevue Hospital. Acceptance there and beginning my nursing career at Bellevue became my next obsession. I knew it would be an uphill battle, but the summer before my last year in high school, hoping for the best, I sent in my application.

For the next six months, I waited for the "We Are Sorry to Inform

You" letter that would put the kibosh on the application or, hopefully, the invitation to New York for the admission interview. Odds were
against me since I didn't shine in math or the sciences, loved English and
languages more, and had no clue how I would ever survive at Bellevue.

But when the prayed for invitation arrived in March, I hoped that
those long hours spent with real patients would overcome all those
obstacles. I left for New York City that morning in March convinced
the path I'd chosen had been the right one. Then came the fateful
fall down the terminal stairs at Port Authority and the interview that
would change my life.

As I limped into the lobby at 440 East 26th Street at ten o'clock
that morning, the three women at the reception desk took one look at
me, sniffed imperiously, and announced, "The Emergency Department
is across the street." Every inch of them shrieked disapproval, from
their stiffly starched white uniforms to the iconic, fluted organdy
Bellevue School of Nursing caps on their carefully coifed heads.

Determined not to cry after what I'd already been through, I faced
them down. I'd done my homework. I knew exactly where it was and
was certain that, if I checked into the Emergency Department first, I'd
be lost there for hours or even days.

"Maybe later," I told them. "I'm here for my nursing school admission interview."

All of them now flustered and fussing over me, one stayed behind to guard the desk, and the other two escorted me down the long
North Wing hallway to the Student Health Center just in time for my
long-anticipated appointment.

To this day, I don't know whether the Director of Health Services
and her staff took pity on me, admired the determination and true
grit it had taken to get me there, or if, at that time and in that place,
Bellevue was where I was meant to be. I'd read *A Lamp Is Heavy* so
often that I'd memorized most of it. Tough enough and determined
enough to ace the application interview and to pick up that lamp, I
would soon learn at Bellevue exactly how heavy it would become.

Chapter Two

BELLEVUE WAS
MY HOME

FROM THE MIDDLE of September 1959 through December 1962, Bellevue was my home. I arrived at 440 East 26th Street at ten o'clock in the morning on September 14, and when I left the day before New Year's Eve three years later, I doubted anyone in my old life would recognize me. Those three years at Bellevue had transformed the shy and uncertain young woman I'd once been into someone who survived the impossible and lived to tell about it.

"Can you believe all this?" I asked another early arrival on Orientation Day in 1959, looking as lost and bewildered as I was. Her name tag said *Kathy B. New York City,* and I wondered, in that huge crowd of new students, if I'd ever see her again.

"It's amazing!" she sighed. "But I only ever saw the Student Health Services Department when I came for my interview."

"Same here," I admitted, remembering that awful day and the certainty I'd lost, in that fall down the stairs at Port Authority Terminal, my only chance at acceptance.

My home away from home for those three life-changing years, "440" was unlike any nursing school I'd ever imagined. Constructed in the early 1950s, almost an entire century after the famous hospital for which it was founded, the nursing school complex extended from First Avenue to East River Drive and one square city block from

Twenty-Fifth to Twenty-Sixth.

I hadn't seen much more than the lobby and Health Services Department during my March interview, but, thanks to *Student Nurse,* which I read over and over those six months before my arrival, I had a general idea of what the Bellevue School of Nursing was all about.

Comprised of three immense wings—the West, which faced First Avenue; the North, which faced the hospital buildings across Twenty-Sixth Street; and the East, which faced the East River—Bellevue School of Nursing had everything. From the pale pink marbled hallways to the large classroom wing, from the swimming pool and two gymnasiums to the Auditorium, 440 was what most of us called our Taj Mahal. Health Services and the Infirmary were in the North Wing. Two cafeterias and multiple meeting rooms were located in the East and North wings, and the male students who attended the Mills School of Nursing occupied the six-story East Wing. The women students in the two classes before we arrived occupied the eleven-story North Wing, and my class, the latest to begin at 440, took over the top ten floors of the West Wing.

I was one of thirty young women assigned to the sixth floor, and my single room looked down onto the tennis courts below. Each room had a closet, a sink, a medicine cabinet, a twin bed tucked against one wall, and a desk and floor lamp against the other. The bathrooms and showers were down the hall at the right center of each floor, and there was a kitchen and lounge at the north end of the hall, before and to the left of the elevators. Any calls we received came into the kiosk opposite the lounge. I lived on the sixth floor, studied there, dreamed there, and eventually thrived there for the thirty-six months it took to complete the program.

Florence Nightingale once wrote, "Hospitals are only an intermediate stage of civilization." Most of us who joined the nursing program that September had never seen anything at all like Bellevue Hospital, the century-old, red-brown brick buildings that had housed multitudes of New York City's desperate, destitute, and often dying patients.

By the beginning of our second week, we were in either the Medical Building (A and B) or in the Surgical Building (L and M), learning how to take care of them, and not all of the 240 members of my class could adapt. My years as a nurse's aide had prepared me for most of what we encountered, and I was not about to give up and go home. I had waited too long for this, and no career other than nursing would satisfy me.

Major changes occurred in the nursing program, beginning with our class of 1962. Our basic education remained the same: we continued to attend classes in Anatomy and Physiology, Chemistry, Microbiology, Nutrition, Nursing Foundations, Psychology, Skills Lab, and Sociology, but would be in the hospital and on the wards sooner than students in the prior classes had been. Additionally, we would perfect our skills in each patient specialty as we studied it: medical patients, as we studied their diagnoses; surgical, as we studied theirs; and all the others as they were introduced in our comprehensive three-year program.

Our student nurse uniforms became more streamlined, and the black shoes and stockings that student nurses had worn for half a century were exchanged for white ones. In the past, first-year students had always worn the starched square cap that denoted their status as the lowest of the lowly "probies" (probationers) who somehow managed to stumble through the first twelve months as students.

The famous fluted, organdy Bellevue cap had been bestowed at the end of the first year, but, with our class, the cap and Bellevue pin would be awarded only at graduation—if we managed to survive that long. Both signified success, and pursuing them made all of us determined to stay the course.

Bellevue School of Nursing had been founded upon Florence Nightingale's precept that "The very first requirement of nursing is that it should do the sick no harm." Considering the two mistakes I made during those first few months, I'm surprised I wasn't handed my walking papers.

During 1959 and early1960, Bellevue Hospital Center had not yet begun to use disposable equipment, and we were required to re-sterilize our metal needles and glass syringes. It was just my bad luck that the tough, little, old man who became my first victim had saddle-leather skin, and the burred needle bent when I attempted to inject his left buttock.

"What the hell! Whaddya think you're doing?" he roared as I apologized and escaped back to the medication room for another syringe and needle.

"Get out of here and leave me alone!" he howled when I failed the second attempt.

This time, the penicillin I drew up from the vial crystallized in the glass syringe on the way back to my patient. "Just shoot me now," I muttered to myself as I went back for that third and final try. "I'm never going to get it, and he'll never let me near him again!"

The instructor that day calmed him down, thanked him for being such a good sport, and gave me some helpful hints on how to prevent any other mishaps. "Don't worry," she told me. "You'll be fine, and you *will* get the hang of it."

I wasn't so sure. Fear of failure loomed, and, for the next few months, I remained miserable and overwhelmed by my coursework and impossible patients on the wards. The me who had been so determined to succeed had disappeared under the weight of all that worry.

Clinical and classroom rotations assigned us to groups that were designated by first initial and last name, so those of us who survived were together for all three years. Not good at studying in groups and pretty much a loner, I studied alone and eventually started spending more time with my fellow "B" classmates after class and on the wards. And then I began to go down to the swimming pool in the evenings. I became reacquainted there with Kathy B., the fellow student I'd met on Orientation Day, and I no longer felt so alone.

Swimming saved me that fall. That and walking everywhere in my exploration of the city I found so fascinating kept me fit and better able to cope with acquiring all the learning skills essential for patient care.

My sister Carroll had already completed the first year as a student nurse at Westchester School of Nursing, and I was just as determined as she was to succeed. That and the fact that I had no Plan B for my life except nursing were great motivators. Besides, I'd left no broken-hearted- boyfriend back home in Pennsylvania, so there was no reason to rush home on weekends. I was eighteen, independent, and not about to say one negative word about my new life to anyone.

There were a few dates that fall, one to Greenwich Village with a Turkish doctor who looked old enough to be my father; another to see *Psycho* with a mortician I met on the bus on a rare trip back to Reading; and another with an NYU student I met at a Friday night party a fellow classmate talked me into attending.

Dating patients wasn't permitted, but I did bend the rules a few times, agreeing to see one of mine after he'd been discharged from the hospital. I had no clue what he saw in me, but I felt sorry for him, a pudgy little man a few years older than I with a gastric ulcer and a look of apprehension that never left him. He reluctantly admitted he was a bookie, took me to see the movie *Sunrise at Campobello* in Times Square, and brought me little gifts of perfume and stockings. After a few months, I stopped hearing from him. I assumed his shady life had caught up with him and mentally wished him well. Determined to survive Bellevue and move on with my life, any more dates with mystery men were just not part of the program.

By the time I went home for vacation the summer after I finished my probationary year, I'd slimmed down, lightened my hair, and become a sophisticated stranger who'd somehow completed all the required courses and clinical rotations, could describe all my adventures that first year in the Big City, and knew that my horizons now extended far beyond Berks County, Pennsylvania.

That vacation lasted two weeks, and then the grueling second year began. As first-year students, we had spent countless hours becoming accustomed to all the realities of life at the famous Bellevue Hospital Center. Now we returned for more hours with actual patients in A and B and L and M, those medical and surgical buildings where most of our patients were admitted. All the medical wards were open, with beds down both left and right walls and head-to-head down the centers of those ancient high-ceilinged wards. There was no privacy and not enough screens to block the view of other patients or anyone walking into the ward.

"Don't forget the ether!" became our rallying cry. One of our biggest problems was all the food stored in bedside stands by patients or their families and the frantic rushes of cockroaches running for their lives as we opened the doors to retrieve bedpans and washbasins. Some students had never even seen a cockroach, but dealing with them soon became part of our preparation for actual patient care. As Bellevue students, it was simply one more hurdle we faced.

Surgical patients in the L and M Building had actual patient cubicles with room for two to four patients each and an occasional private room for infected isolation patients. One of the first bed baths I ever provided as a student nurse occurred in L and M, to a twenty-year-old prisoner of the City of New York, handcuffed to his bed rail with a police guard not too far away.

"You like what you see, sweet thing?" he asked as I pulled back the top sheet and began bathing him. I was eighteen. I'd never seen a naked man, much less one who smirked every minute it took to complete the bed bath. Flushed a fiery red, speechless with embarrassment, I forged ahead, determined to survive every curve thrown at me in this strange new world I found myself in.

That first summer, as beginning second-year students, we suffered from New York City's unbearable heat. As immaculate as we were when we walked across the street from 440 to the hospital entrance, our starched blue and white uniforms, bibs, and aprons became as bedraggled as we were as soon as we arrived. Built in the 1850s, those wards at Bellevue were high-ceilinged and hot as hell, with not a single air conditioner or fan in sight.

Each of us spent endless hours in Med-Surg that summer, seasoned students now. Those hours have blended together in my memory, but what stands out is that I preferred male patients to females (who complained about anything and everything) and all the long hours we spent doing bed baths, giving enemas, and every other task we were required to perform, with absolutely no privacy for anyone.

Surgical Services provided more drama and excitement than Medical, and one day, my patient, hemorrhaging like Old Faithful from an iliac artery repair, provided even more. "Keep your hands on that bleeder!" the intern on duty called out as he, the orderly, and I, desperately holding pressure with my hands on that bleeder, raced with him, out cold and oblivious, from his fourth-floor cubicle, down the corridors into an ancient elevator and up to the Operating Rooms on the ninth floor. Incredibly, the man survived an episode equal to any I'd ever seen on television's *Dr. Kildare* or *Ben Casey, MD.*

That second year, I continued nightly trips down to the swimming pool, studied harder than ever, and began writing as a staff writer and assistant editor for our school paper, *Starch and Stripes,* which provided a much-needed balance between the realities of 440 and the intense new world I inhabited.

In December, I reconnected with Drew, a young man with whom I'd grown up in New York before moving at fourteen to Pennsylvania. We dated off and on, and I visited him at his college in Upstate New York, but neither of us envisioned any kind of future together. As young adults, we were far different than we'd been as children, and by then I had my heart set on completing the program at Bellevue and heading on out to California, where my mother had gone at eighteen.

During those three years at Bellevue, we were not allowed to have jobs. Some of us received small allowances for basic essentials, but many depended on babysitting to get us through, and there were plenty of opportunities for that. Mostly, we were referred by word of mouth. Students would pass on requests from clients to other students who wanted to babysit, or calls would come in to the front desk in our lobby from those looking for babysitters. Fortunately, there were no limits to those requests. Most of us walked down First Avenue past Twenty-Third Street and babysat in the never-ending complex called Stuyvesant Town. I took jobs wherever they came up and thought nothing of venturing all the way down to Washington Square, west across town toward Central Park, and as far north as Harlem.

Weeknights, we had to be back at 440 by midnight, but, on the weekends, we could stay out later. With a dollar as our usual rate for every sitting we job accepted, we kept ourselves in spending money. This was late 1960 and early 1961. A dollar an hour was fine with me. My ending salary at St. Joseph's in Reading had been just fifty cents an hour.

Babysitting jobs became a godsend. They got me out of 440 when the stress of constant studying overwhelmed me. In my ranging alone all over the city, I never had a problem with safety, made sure to look as if I always knew where I was going, and always managed to get back to 440 without any problems.

In 1959, the total cost of a nursing education at Bellevue was $200. The School of Nursing paid each student a monthly stipend to cover the cost of books and new nursing shoes when we wore out the old ones. That stipend went into our student accounts. What remained at the end of three years was turned over to us.

My mother sent me a small allowance that first year. Eternally grateful, I asked her to stop sending it as soon as babysitting jobs became plentiful and I could be on my own. Then, toward the end of my second year, another option to cover my personal expenses presented itself.

When I learned about the Army Student Nurse Program from a recruiter who had come to 440 to tell us about it, I decided to apply right away. It supported selected student nurses from across the country through the final year of our nursing programs. As Private E-1s, we would receive a check for $78 per month until graduation, and, upon RN licensure, we would report to the Medical Field School at Fort Sam Houston, Texas, for orientation as second lieutenants in the Army Nurse Corps Reserves. That option was too tempting to turn down, but because I wasn't yet twenty-one, my parents had to provide their consent. My father had reservations about any of his daughters entering the military. "Absolutely not!" he told me the first time it came up. "You didn't go off to New York two years ago just to end up in the Army!"

But my mother, who'd had a few adventures of her own before marrying my dad, was a hundred percent behind me, so, when I brought it up again a week later, my dad reluctantly agreed to provide permission. No one else in my class wanted to join, so I followed in the footsteps of a senior classmate a year ahead of me and, in August 1961, was inducted into the Army Student Nurse Program at Ft. Jay, Governor's Island, with no idea where I'd go from there or where my Army career would take me.

I loved that entire day at Fort Jay, the tour of the post just a stone's throw from the Statue of Liberty in New York Harbor and all the attention that I and my colleague, Betty Ann, from rival nursing school St. Vincent's, received. We had a tour of the post and lunch at the Officers' Mess. A few months later, one of the soldiers from a unit in Germany sent me a bottle of Chanel N°5. after seeing our photo in the latest issue of the military's *Stars and Stripes*.

By that summer, we all completed week after week of additional clinical education in the Medical and Surgical wards and spent the required months in most of the specialties in our extensive and exhaustive program, including the Operating Room, Obstetrics, Pediatrics, all the specialty clinics, Rehabilitation Nursing, and Psychiatry. All were memorable, especially Obstetrics, where the Resident, Dr. Montalvo, stepped back as the baby's head was crowning and said to me, "It's your turn, Nurse Barbara. Go ahead and deliver this little kiddo."

Learning about it and actually doing it were completely different, but this was the young mother's third child, the delivery was uncomplicated, and the baby girl soon arrived, slippery, screaming her little head off, and landing safely in my waiting hands. As terrified as I'd been, this is a memory of my Bellevue years that I'll never forget.

Psychiatry was provided at Bellevue's famous Psychiatric Hospital, located at First Avenue and Thirtieth Street, the site of countless movies and television programs where people who acted weirdly or dangerously were "hauled off to Bellevue for observation." Psychiatry Service was intended to house up to six hundred inpatients but usually had a census of up to a thousand. It had a court for psychiatric hearings and was the triage site for patients committed to the multitudes of psychiatric facilities throughout New York State.

I spent my three-month rotation at the Thirtieth Street facility in the Male Semi-Disturbed and Female Adolescent Services. The young females were there primarily for societal reasons, but the men had diagnoses ranging from bipolar affect to schizophrenia.

Dealing with the men who often just needed someone to listen wasn't a problem, but our instructor, a bird-like little woman afraid of her own shadow, thought we'd all be far better off away from them and sequestered safely in the unit office. "You'll be fine here," she twittered as she left us in the office and went out to find suitable patients for us to care for. It made for an interesting, strange, and frustrating month in that portion of my rotation.

I look back on those twelve months of my second year with nostalgia, not for the endless hours we spent in our clinical rotations but for the unforgettable highlights: an agitated man in Psychiatry who came after me after I innocently beat him at shuffleboard; the first day in the OR when I carried away a patient's amputated leg; the patient in the Neurology Unit who always seemed to have grand mal seizures on days I was assigned to care for him.

I remember the butterballs covered in sugar and the Coke syrup we fed to our renal failure patients so as not to overwhelm them with protein; the old-fashioned metal steamed-food carts that we pushed up and down those open wards, delivering meals to our patients; the glass IV solution bottles that we recycled as drainage containers for urine or bile. We seldom wore gloves, our equipment was rarely sterile, and it was a real wonder that neither students nor long-suffering patients succumbed to overwhelming sepsis.

That second year ended with associate editorship, then editorship of *Starch and Stripes* for my final year. And when I went home for my two-week vacation that June, I knew I'd be going back for increasing hours in Medical and Surgical patient care and, as a senior now, staffing the hospital with my fellow classmates when nursing staffs took their summer vacations. Twenty years old, I had survived the worst and the best of what Bellevue had thrown at me and was ready to go the distance.

Chapter Three

"DO THE SICK NO HARM"

IN *BELLEVUE IS My Home,* Dr. Cutolo made the medical center seem magical and mystical to a seventeen-year-old set on a career in nursing. He'd dedicated his book to "the men and women who have given to Bellevue their minds, their hands and their hearts." By the end of my second year, mysticism remained, but the magic had long since gone. We had survived so far through sheer grit and determination. Being a Bellevue nurse meant hard work and more of it the closer we came to our graduation in June.

The Army Student Nurse Program required only that I maintain my grades and report any changes in my student status. Those grades improved, and though it added one more element of stress, editorship of *Starch and Stripes* balanced the onslaught of information we absorbed as we continued through our clinical rotations. I loved working on the newspaper and looked forward to the monthly trips down to Manhattan's lower East Side to the print shop where we set it up for publication.

Florence Nightingale's imperative that nurses stand when attending physicians entered the room and remained obsequious or silent in their presence still held true in the 1960s. However, that didn't hold true for the medical students, interns, and residents with whom we interacted on a daily basis.

Bellevue Medical Center was affiliated with four medical schools, both New York University Medical and Post-Graduate Medical Schools, Columbia University, and Cornell, and during the years I was a student nurse, and for many years after, medical students, interns, and residents learned right along with us. By the time we were experienced seniors, we knew a great deal more about patient care and the nursing process than they did, but the real difference was that all information and experiences were shared, and there was an ongoing sense of esprit de corps. With no technological monitoring in those days, we learned by seat-of—he-pants experience and pure instinct which patients would "go bad"; we worked tirelessly to care for them; and we learned what it really meant to Do the Sick No Harm.

After the Christmas holidays, my senior classmates and I started concentrating on the areas in which we planned to focus during those last six months before graduation. We continued our endless rotations through the Medical and Surgical services, and coming up fast was the decision where to spend the ten weeks of Senior Focus.

I'd been considering Operating Room, which I thoroughly enjoyed during my two-month rotation, but Perioperative nursing was still in its infancy, with far too little actual interaction between nurses and sedated or anesthetized patients. I would miss that, and, besides, my sister Carroll, recently graduated from Westchester School of Nursing, had chosen Operating Room for her first assignment, and I knew I'd need to forge ahead in a different direction. From childhood into my early twenties, I'd taken on the most daunting challenges. Bellevue was one of them; choosing to spend the ten-week senior focus in Chest Service was another. I'd already completed the required two-week rotation through D-3, the dreaded Medical Chest Service Admitting unit, and, to my surprise, had actually liked it.

Medical students, interns, and residents in the evolving specialty of Pulmonary Medicine rotated there, and, for all of us, it was an intense learning experience. One entire ward of twenty beds was devoted to tuberculosis, prevalent in our area of the Lower East Side of

Manhattan. Gowning up and masking in order to safely care for those patients quickly became routine, and by the end of those two weeks on D-3, tuberculosis held no terrors for me.

We also cared for patients with tumors, pulmonary emboli, emphysema—also known as Chronic Obstructive Pulmonary Disease—and a plethora of respiratory system infections. By far the most terrifying segment of the initial two weeks was the large open room of the D-3 hallway in which seven iron lungs operated continuously. Used originally for the patients who'd survived polio but required respiratory support, they were also now used for patients with cervical spine injuries who couldn't breathe on their own. On a rotating basis, they were frequently used for the emphysema patients who didn't respond well to the Bird or Bennet IPPBs—Intermittent Positive Pressure Breathing machines.

My fellow classmates thought I'd lost what was left of my mind when I chose to return to D-3 for my senior focus, and even more insane when I decided to take my first position there as a new graduate nurse after we'd completed our thirty-six-month program in September. "That place is the worst! All those tuberculosis patients and iron lungs! D-3 is tough enough, but patient care through those portholes! I'll take a job anywhere but there!" one told me on a day when we'd been talking about our lives after we'd survived as students. In all the years since then, those months spent on D-3 have been the most intense, the most trying, and, ultimately, the most satisfying I ever spent in hands-on patient care.

The most noteworthy events for us as seniors were our two graduation ceremonies in June 1962: the capping, pinning, and graduation at Bellevue School of Nursing, followed by our graduation the next day with all the colleges of New York University with which our school was affiliated.

For the Bellevue graduation, we wore the crisply starched, white, multi-buttoned, and long-sleeved ceremonial Bellevue uniforms, white stockings, and white shoes. As our names were called, we walked across the stage in the 440 auditorium to be capped and pinned by the Director of Nursing with the iconic emblems that distinguished all Bellevue graduates for the past one hundred years.

The next day, the 178 of us, in our elegant white uniforms and wearing our caps and pins, rose together as the Bellevue School Nursing Class of 1962 graduated with all the schools associated with New York University.

After all that acclamation and glory, it was tough to come back to reality, but come back we did, wearing the blue-and-white-striped, white bibbed and aproned uniforms we'd all worn as students, and also wearing the caps and pins that signified our success. For the next three months, everyone would know we were the new graduates. We'd made it, and, if we could do it, so could the new juniors and seniors who followed right behind us.

Once again, we went back to the wards where we'd first learned what it really meant to be Bellevue nurses, rotating through days, evenings, and nights, and staffing the medical center the last summer we would be there. I didn't mind the 8:00 a.m. to 4:30 p.m. or the 4:00 p.m. to 12:30 a.m. shifts, but absolutely hated the midnight to 8:00 a.m. shift. Unable to sleep days and work nights through that unbearably hot New York summer, I vowed *never to work another night shift unless I absolutely had to.*

Ironically, decades after leaving Bellevue, I spent more than thirty years of my career in nursing doing just that, working eight, ten, or twelve-hour night shifts in Emergency, Critical Care, Administrative Supervision, Oncology, and back again to Med-Surg and Progressive Care. Those years between had made a difference. Now I actually preferred the shift that focused on patient care, had far less interference from nursing administration or physicians, and left more free time during daylight hours to pursue other interests.

That last summer in New York, I spent as much off-duty time as possible on the roof of the East Wing, working on my suntan and watching the small boats and larger ships as they navigated up and down the busy East River. I also met and dated Tom, an older man of twenty-nine, just as disinterested as I was in a lasting relationship. In six months, I'd be heading for Texas and the Army Nurse Corps. Nothing and no one could keep me in New York. Even then, so early in my career, I lived in a perpetual future.

In September, I moved from the sixth floor in the West Wing to the tenth floor in the North. My room, identical to the one I'd lived in as a student nurse, faced directly across Twenty-Sixth Street to C and D Buildings, where I'd spend the next three months as charge nurse on D-3. That was also where, day after day and night after night, ambulances raced up and down that narrow street, picking up and dropping off patients at the perpetually swamped Emergency Department. All of us who lived and worked there soon got used to the incessant wail of sirens.

Once again, I was re-inventing myself, suspended between student life and the one waiting for me in the Army. In November, all the new graduate nurses in New York State would take the Registered Nurse Licensing Exam, offered once each year and a huge source of anxiety for us. I doubted that the Army would wait for me to take it again, and I'd be mortified if I failed.

And so, from September until the middle of November, my mornings were spent studying for the exam and my evenings from 4:00 p.m. until 2:00 a.m. (I never got off duty at midnight in those three months I spent on D-3), learning my craft on Bellevue's Chest Service. I would report to the unit at 4:00 p.m., plan how to care for the patients assigned, then head to the cafeteria to bolt down an early dinner. I was the only graduate nurse on the unit, the only one to take charge, to medicate the patients, and to assist all the physicians coming and going during the shift, so the preponderance of patient care fell on me.

Nothing had changed since Senior Focus. I still had the full ward of twenty tubercular patients, still had those seven iron lungs running continuously, still had a census of thirty-five to forty patients at any given time, many of them critically ill. I spent most of each shift moving the ones more terminally ill to the beds in the rooms on either side of the glassed-in nurses' station in order to observe them more closely. I could count on at least one death each shift. There were no cardiac monitors, no CPR, and nursing care was done on the run. Our attending physicians, students from four medical schools, interns and residents came and went at all hours, so I had to be available to assist with all the procedures and treatments that were ordered.

Patient charting hardly ever happened before change of shift at midnight, and, more often than not, I saved mine until after the night shift nurse had taken over. Frequently, as short staffed as Bellevue usually was, I worked an extra ten-hour shift each week, and by the time the two-day licensing exam occurred in November, I decided that three months as a new graduate would be the last at Bellevue, or I wouldn't survive long enough to see Fort Sam Houston, Texas.

I volunteered to work through all the holidays that year, and my final days on D-3 were bittersweet. I managed to survive some of the most demanding experiences as a student nurse and even more daunting ones as a new graduate. Not even the terrifying Cuban Missile Crisis that October, with Russian nuclear weapons aimed directly at New York, had slowed me down. In another three months, I'd be on my way to Texas. There was absolutely nothing left of that awkward and uncertain eighteen-year-old who had left home and begun her nursing career at Bellevue a lifetime ago.

Chapter Four

ARMY DAZE

THE TWELVE MONTHS after leaving Bellevue were the twelve most significant months of my life. I spent the first two of them with my parents in Reading, Pennsylvania. In order to pass the time and keep those hard-won nursing skills current, I accepted a position in Emergency at St. Joseph's Hospital. My high school years as a nurse's aide there had been invaluable at Bellevue, and returning as a shining new nurse after my graduation was a debt I was determined to repay. That job was a godsend, but while I loved the challenges I faced every shift in Emergency, it had become a little uncomfortable at home. No longer the tentative fledgling who had left the nest in 1959, I was a determined-to-be-independent twenty-one-year-old with three years of growing up behind me. My sisters Carroll and Jeanie were still on the East Coast. The Army was the destiny I would fashion for myself in an entirely new part of the country. I already knew that after two months of orientation at Fort Sam Houston, Texas, most of my assignments would be nowhere near Reading, Pennsylvania, and my parents accepted the fact that I would rarely be back.

What complicated those first two months of 1963 were my self-doubts, wavering over what would happen in Texas, and where I would go from there. Carroll was now married, had her first daughter, and seemed satisfied with her life. Jeanie was eighteen and still living at home. I began dating again, a man from Reading whom I'd met the year before. He asked me to marry him and accept all that he had to offer in that suburban city in Eastern Pennsylvania, but I turned him down. I was determined to pursue my own destiny, whatever that was, and I wasn't in love with him. I did want to fall in love with someone, and I knew it wouldn't be fair to either of us to start a new life with him and to always wonder what might have been.

Nursing in that small Emergency Department meant hands-on care based only on what I observed and what my patients revealed to me. There were no Board-Certified Emergency physicians, no cardiac monitoring, and no CPR. The tragic loss of a patient who hemorrhaged after an attending physician transected an artery while performing a tracheostomy haunted me for weeks. I knew I needed more than what St. Joseph's had to offer and waited anxiously to receive those New York State Board of Nursing results.

By the first week in March, I was finally set to go. My trunk was packed and ready, and I had no last-minute doubts. When the State Board results and my orders to report to the Medical Field Service School, Ft. Sam Houston, Texas, arrived on the same day, I'd already mentally left Reading, Pennsylvania, far behind.

Like most first-class adventures, mine began in the middle of a snowstorm, a perfect way to leave that old life behind and start a new one. Trains had always been an exciting element of my childhood, so taking one from Reading to Hershey, from Hershey to St. Louis, and then from St. Louis to San Antonio seemed the best way to begin that new life.

My parents took me to dinner that last Friday evening in Reading. I was due to report in at the Medical Field Service School on Monday, and, although this would be the last time I would see them for who knew how long, boarding that train and finally being on my way was all I could think about.

Sleet and snow still whipped and whirled around me as I detrained at Hershey and took a cab to the Baltimore and Ohio terminal for the second leg of the journey. Once aboard in Hershey, I settled into that snug little roomette—a single compartment with sink, commode, and fold-down seat-to-bed—and fell asleep to the clacking of the wheels as we sped through the night through Pennsylvania into Ohio.

Breakfast and lunch were served in the dining car, reminiscent of scenes from one of my favorite movies, *North by Northwest.* To add to the adventure, I met some fascinating fellow travelers as our train made its steady progress across the country toward Missouri. One of them was a tall, good-looking Army Specialist First Class who commiserated with the rest of us on Saturday afternoon when we learned that, because of the late start in Hershey, we would arrive too late in St. Louis to make ongoing connections. He was on his way to Oakland, California, a designated military escort for the remains of one of his fellow soldiers who had tragically died in a training accident. I was on my way to Ft. Sam, a soon-to-be officer. He was enlisted. It didn't matter to either of us that, in the insular world of the Army, we probably never would have met. Polite and respectful, he was a godsend in getting me and my luggage to the St. Louis hotel that the railroad assigned to us, calling out as we left the train in St. Louis, "Excuse me, ma'am, but could you use some help?"

That respectful "ma'am" absolutely charmed me. He couldn't have been much older than I was. Someone had taught him impeccable manners, and he was nothing at all like the young men I'd met so far in my relatively short life. "I'd like that," I told him, no longer interested in being Little Miss Independent.

It was an innocent Saturday evening and Sunday morning, and I knew, when we said goodbye at the terminal where we were to catch our respective trains, that I'd probably never see him again.

On the last leg of the journey, from Sunday morning to early Monday afternoon, I enjoyed the train ride and my last meal on board, this time with a courtly elderly gentleman, intrigued by my stories about Bellevue, New York City, and the upcoming introduction to the Army Nurse Corps.

Departure from Reading, Pennsylvania, and arrival in San Antonio, Texas, couldn't have been more different. Blustering wind and snow on the East Coast and blistering heat and sun in the Southwest were almost too much to understand, and I soon realized that packing only cold weather clothing in my suitcase and sending all my other clothes ahead in a trunk had not been the best plan after all. San Antonio on that first Monday in March was worse than all those sizzling summer days in New York City had ever been. I arrived there at 1400 hours military time, took a cab to the Billeting Office at Fort Sam Houston, and then took another one across the post to the multi-storied BOQ, Bachelor Officers' Quarters, adjacent to Brooke Army Medical Center.

My single room, larger than the ones at Bellevue's 440, looked more comfortable than I expected, but the entire building was much too silent. The officer candidates in the orientation class ahead of mine were either in class, on duty at BAMC, or had already left for their next duty assignments. The officer candidate who would share the adjacent bathroom with me hadn't yet arrived, and, unexpectedly, I started feeling a little bit lonely.

That didn't last long. Before I found the energy to unpack, a call came in from Walter, a fellow classmate at the Bellevue-Mills School of Nursing who'd been in the Army for the past two months, enlisting from New York after he received his nursing license exam results. He'd been a friend of many of us in the class of 1962, and it was great to see him and to learn firsthand what to expect at Fort Sam. He took me to dinner off-post that night, and we got together a few more times before he left Fort Sam for his first duty assignment.

By then, I'd become caught up in the whirlwind of officers' training, more committed to surviving Fort Sam than to any actual social life. Our Tactical Officer, who taught close order drill every morning, despaired that any of us would ever master those marches around the Quad at MFSS, the Medical Field Service School. We shared our classrooms with several other officer candidates in their medical specialist services. One, an entomologist in the Medical Specialist Corps, caught my eye, but neither of us conquered our shyness long enough to become acquainted.

Before that first month ended, I bought my first car, a snappy little red and white Ford Falcon, and spent whatever free time available perfecting East Coast driving skills on those endless San Antonio suburban highways. And just to prove that nothing in this new life in the Army could stop me, I decided to try something I had never in my wildest dreams considered.

When several fellow classmates mentioned learning how to ride horseback into those wide-open spaces around Fort Sam Houston, I thought, *Why not?* None of us had ever ridden, most had never been anywhere near a horse, but we trooped over to the riding school run by a retired Army Cavalry Major and signed up for what would become the most exciting, most uncomfortable experience we would have during our orientation.

"Now, y'all listen up!" he told us before we got up onto our assigned rides. "The only way to stay on and not fall off is to grip your horse's sides with your knees, and don't let loose of those reins!"

Tough and exacting, the Major took us out on endless rides across that long parade ground and out into dry and dusty Texas countryside. No Western saddles for us—the Major taught us to ride with English saddles, and, just as he'd told us, using only our knees and our hands to hold on. He and I shared a birthday. On March 15th, he turned seventy and I turned twenty-two, grateful that, so far, I'd survived those early morning rides.

Although we did learn to ride, walking, sitting down, and all those endless close order drills around the Quad after our hours with the Major became excruciating ordeals, and, as a group, we decided we'd had enough of life in the saddle. On that last ride out, I decided to give up horses forever when the one I'd been riding flipped me over his head, looked down disdainfully at me in the dust, and pranced away. I'd been put painfully in my place and ended up at BAMC for a spinal X-ray to rule out a herniated disc.

Orientation to the Army was tougher than any of us ever antic-ipated. Along with our long-suffering Tactical Officer, we suspected we'd never learn those close-order drills and were the laughingstock of the Medical Field Service School as we stumbled and fumbled our way around the Quad every morning at 0700 during that first month at Fort Sam.

But if close order drill was bad, our weeklong bivouac out to Camp Bullis was worse and almost ended Army orientation for a lot of us. Our instructors transported us out there to the wilds of Texas on a rickety, ramshackle old Army bus on a Monday afternoon, the second week in April. At barely a hundred pounds, I looked like Beetle Baily in BDUs (battle dress uniforms). My combat boots were too big, the soft camo cap covered my hair and most of my face, and dog tags on a chain around my neck clanked against my olive-drab T-shirt when-ever I moved. We all looked pitiful. It didn't help that the heat that week was especially oppressive or that none of us believed we'd survive Camp Bullis after we saw the caterpillars.

I'd easily become accustomed to the cockroaches at Bellevue, since they were just one more component of patient care in one of New York City's oldest hospitals. But the caterpillars in Texas were an entirely different story. Thousands of them fell from the trees, onto the ground, and all over our Army issue cots, covering everything in their path like a creepy, crawly, constantly moving carpet.

The last straw was watching them fall through the roof of the canvas mess tent, onto the tables and chairs and into the steam ta-bles, which held the food for our evening meals. Even the Army brass thought it was too much for anyone to take and bussed us all back to our quarters at Fort Sam that first afternoon. We did return the next day, much to our dismay, and stuck it out at Camp Bullis for the rest of the week. We were caterpillar-free but covered in dust and sweat, learning from the ground up what life would be like in a Mobile Army Surgical Hospital once we survived our two-month officer orientation and received our transfer orders.

MASH, BAMC, MFSS, FSHT—those initials and what they symbolized (Mobile Army Surgical Hospital; Brooke Army Medical Center; Medical Field Service School; Fort Sam Houston Texas) were burned into our brains that week in the wild and in the remaining eight weeks we'd been assigned to orientation. I could rattle them off easily, and, to this day, can still recite that Army ID number.

By now, things were about to change on a personal level. Finally, pretty impressively, we learned how to march in perfect formation all around the Quad every morning at 0700. Except for two classmates who had caught the eye of two married officers on TDY, temporary duty, at Fort Sam, we hadn't met many men. But on the Easter weekend after we survived Camp Bullis, two of my classmates and I struck gold.

That Saturday night, April 13, a dietitian from Colorado, a nurse classmate from Upstate New York, and I ran into three non-commissioned National Guard enlistees from California at Brooke Army Medical Center for corpsman training. Against regulations, they were at the out-of-bounds Pit, a bar on post open only to officers and their guests.

My classmate took a liking to the pharmacist from Los Angeles, the dietitian hooked up with a would-be actor from Hollywood, and I ended up with the pharmacist from the Salinas Valley, California. That night, for all of us, Army Orientation took second place. And for me, it was fascination at first sight. *Thunderbolt City!* I thought as soon as the soldier from California said hello.

"You're from New York?" he asked. "Really? I've never met anyone from there."

"And I've never met anyone from California!"

David had the most astonishing eyes, the palest, icy blue and slightly slanted at the corners. It was inevitable that I fell for him, tall and tan, three years older and just as shy as I was. The fact that he and his buddies were hanging out in the sacrosanct Pit made meeting them that much better. We three couples spent as much time together as we could during the week and on weekends away from Fort Sam. The last thing on our minds was completing orientation. I vaguely remember mine, the classes at MFSS and the hours we spent on the wards at BAMC that were surprisingly like the ones where I'd spent so much time at Bellevue.

Exhausted by those weekends away, I made it through the remainder of our Army Nurse Corps Orientation in a fog. This was my first real honest-to-God adventure, unlike any other in the years since leaving home, and a whole new fearless, brave, and daring side of me emerged.

I knew it had to end, that this good-looking California man with the amazing eyes would be leaving soon for his home in the Salinas Valley, and I would be receiving orders for my next assignment. I was positive it would be the end of us, but I was wrong. David was as infatuated with me as I was with him, and when I told him I'd received orders to report to Madigan General Hospital in Washington State two weeks after graduation, he asked, "Would you like me to make the trip as far as California with you?"

The New York nurse and the Los Angeles pharmacist went back home to their respective lives, the Colorado dietitian and would-be actor went to Hollywood and got married, and David and I headed west together. Infatuated with each other, we made that trip together from Texas to California, and, on the way, we fell in love. He was my first real lover. I was as besotted with him as he was intrigued with me, and when we became engaged on that epic journey, our lives changed forever.

My parents, who met on a bus heading for the East Coast in 1939 and got married in Reno three days later, were nevertheless alarmed when we called from Palm Springs to announce our engagement. His parents were horrified that he'd chosen a New Yorker/Army Nurse/ Alien Life Form who had seduced their younger son. They were even more upset when they learned that not only would he not be staying home in Salinas, he would be moving with me to Tacoma to live while

I completed my first duty assignment at Madigan.

David would remain in Salinas for the next few weeks, tying up the loose ends of his life, and I would drive on to Fort Lewis to begin my assignment at Madigan Army Medical Center at the end of May. He gave me an emerald engagement ring; we spent a few days with his older brother Bill and his family in Sacramento, and then I headed out to Interstate 5 for the first leg of my journey. I was on my own, driving my new car out of California, through Oregon and on to Fort Lewis, Washington, that huge military post just outside Tacoma.

As long and lonely as that drive had been, I enjoyed all of it until the first night in my motel somewhere between Ashland and Medford, Oregon. I showered and started to dry my hair when whoosh!—out went the power in the entire motel. The culprit was the hairdryer that had begun to sputter and spark as soon as I plugged it in.

"When has any part of my Army adventure ever been boring?" I asked myself. As it turned out, the electrical outlet had a prior checkered history, and it was just my bad luck to rent that room where it blew out all the power.

Already exhausted by the long drive and rattled by that power outage, I called David, still in Sacramento with his brother and family, and played it all down. "Remember that song 'The Night the Lights Went Out in Georgia'? Well, they went out in Oregon too, and I'm lucky my hair didn't catch fire! The wall socket shorted out and—"

"You had to be there when it happened. Just be careful! I'm counting on you to be alive at our wedding!" We laughed as he said it, but, three weeks later, I started wondering if this new life of mine would even last that long.

A week before David was due to come to Tacoma to drive with me back to Sacramento for the wedding, I almost did myself in again, and this time it was all my fault. I'd just left Tacoma on the way back to my apartment in Lakeland after a final fitting for my wedding dress. Distracted by all the things yet to be done, happy to be seeing David again, I tossed my half-smoked cigarette out the car window. I thought

I'd stubbed it out. I shouldn't have thrown it out it in the first place, but it flew back and into the back seat of my car and set a stack of folded laundry on fire.

There I was, racing down the freeway on the outskirts of Tacoma, Washington, with the back seat of my new, little, red Falcon on fire, trying find a safe place to stop and praying that I could get the fire out before I became a living torch. "Somebody help me!" I screamed as I roared into the open space at the far-left side of the Chevron station just off the freeway, away from the pumps and any other vehicles, and ran over to the two attendants who had watched me drive in.

"My car's on fire!" I cried, as if they couldn't see it for themselves. That stack of laundry I'd washed, folded, and hadn't packed away was ruined, and the back seat, pulled out of the car by my two rescuers, was a burned-out wreck.

"Don't even ask!" I told them. "I feel bad enough already. And so stupid. But thank you for saving my life! I'm supposed to be getting married next week!"

They probably thought 'Poor guy!' and they would have been right. I was no prize, and I told David so when I called him that night. "You've still got time to call it off. Run while you can! I'm nothing but trouble, and your mother will be relieved to see the end of me!"

"You're not getting away from me *now!*" he laughed. "Besides, I'd kind of like to see what comes next." That should have been our warning.

And so, with nothing else to go wrong—except for the four wisdom teeth that the Army dentist decided had to come out that week before the wedding—we were married that last week in June 1963. The small ceremony was held in the auditorium of a Catholic school in the city where his older brother and family lived, with them, his parents, my mother, and a small cluster of nuns in attendance. The priest who married us was a colleague of the priest at Fort Lewis with whom I'd taken Catholic instruction. Both had originally been from New York, and, years before, both had attended the same seminary in Westchester

County, where I'd grown up.

We had a magical California honeymoon and moved into the apartment in Lakewood, close to Fort Lewis and McCord Air Force Base. At the end of July, we learned I was pregnant. David had mumps as a teenager and had been warned that children might never happen. We were both surprised then thrilled at the pregnancy, and I thought I could remain in the Army, have our baby, and still complete my two-year obligation.

At that time, none of the military services permitted female personnel with children to remain on active duty. It never occurred to me that the pregnancy would be a problem, but once the Army obstetrician confirmed that a baby was on the way, my superior officer informed me that I'd be honorably discharged by the end of the year. I was disappointed at the news, but knew that my husband, who had gamely changed his life and followed me all the way up to Washington, would be happy.

He would work as a pharmacist in Auburn, a rural city north of Seattle, and I would begin my assignment in the newborn nursery at Madigan, since the Chief Nurse had decided that my original assignment in Intensive Care might be harmful to my advancing pregnancy. I was happy in my marriage and thrilled about the baby. Then the unimaginable happened.

I was on duty that unbelievable week in November when President Kennedy was killed in Dallas, and we were as appalled as everyone at the events that held us in thrall through the end of that terrible week. December could not come soon enough.

On active duty in the Army for only ten months in 1963, my life changed radically from the night I left Reading, Pennsylvania, and arrived in the blazing sun of San Antonio, Texas. In the blink of an eye, I was in Tacoma, Washington, with a husband I scarcely knew and a baby on the way. What the hell had happened? My longed for career in the Army ended before it had really begun, and I had no idea where we, as a family, would go from there.

Chapter Five

CALIFORNIA DREAMING

OUR FIRST DAUGHTER was born at Madigan Army Medical Center in April 1964. We named her Laura Mary, after both grandmothers, and had to learn how to become instant parents. Because I'd been an officer, I was provided with a private room with rooming-in for her, a good thing for all the other mothers in the open ward, whose babies slept serenely in their cribs next to them. From the start, mine was the first to wake up and the first to scream soundly for her feedings and diaper changes.

My husband had rarely been around babies, and while I had cared for quite a few at Bellevue and in the Newborn Nursery at Madigan, this little creature was ours, and caring for her became a constant challenge. From the beginning, David was tentative with her. Some of that hesitancy was because she was so tiny and so needy, but I suspected that part of him resented the fact that he was no longer the only love in my life. Going out of my way to reassure him, it felt like I had two children who needed all my attention.

Somehow, we managed and started making plans to leave Washington. I loved it there, despite the rain, but my husband missed his home in the Salinas Valley, and that year away had been hard on him. I also wanted to continue our married lives in California, so leaving all my military connections behind wasn't a problem. California dreaming began for us the April that Laura was born, and, by June 1964, we were on our way.

Having a new baby meant not returning to nursing, but, in planning for the move to California, I began thinking about it. Once we were settled, maybe I would apply for a position, at least on a part-time basis. But first my husband had to find a job. This was a fresh start for both of us, and, at first, we set our sights on Santa Barbara. Unfortunately, there were no open positions for pharmacists there at the time, but David heard about the need for a hospital pharmacist in Ventura County, fifty miles to the south. That was a small community facility in Oxnard, and since they needed an RN as well as a pharmacist, we decided to stay.

David would work a full-time day shift, and, once I completed orientation, I would work part-time evenings. When he returned home at 6 p.m., he would relieve the babysitter, and I'd take over once I finished my shift at 11 p.m. I knew he resented having to care for a frequently crying baby and having to wait up for me when he wanted to sleep. More than once I had to remind him what we had agreed to when he asked that I take a part-time job to help with all our expenses. "It's just two evening shifts a week. Laura will sleep after the babysitter feeds her and gives her a bedtime bottle. I just need you to be here for her if she wakes up and starts to cry."

By mid-June 1964, we'd been able to find a small apartment within walking distance of the hospital so we could return home quickly if we were needed, and, with the issue of part-time babysitting still not entirely decided, we had settled into our new home and our new careers.

St. John's was typical of small community hospitals throughout the country, with private practitioners serving as attending physicians but with no interns or residents and no training programs for nurses or physicians. With four medical schools in affiliation at Bellevue, I'd become accustomed to the valuable medical educational adjuncts to my own excellent nursing program that they provided.

Private physicians were often difficult to deal with at St. John's, and, at that time, nurses still stood at attention when they walked in and still stayed silent unless they asked us to speak. In the middle of 1964, we had most of the medical specialties, but CPR hadn't been fully utilized. Intensive Care meant only rudimentary bedside monitoring, and Emergency Medicine meant that any available physician who could be talked into it would take a shift or two. There were no Critical Care or Emergency Medicine Board Certifications. Most nurses interested in Intensive Care took basic arrhythmia recognition classes and monitored patients, one or two at a time, in large open rooms with basic monitoring at the bedside for each patient.

Because of my experiences in St. Joseph's Hospital Emergency Department before I'd left Reading for the Army and those challenging shifts survived on D-3 before leaving Bellevue in December 1962, nursing administration at St. John's in Oxnard thought I'd be a good fit for the Emergency Department.

Three memorable events occurred during my few short months there: a young man was stabbed; an older man was critically burned; and I had an infuriating confrontation with the ED physician that cost me my first nursing position in California.

That first summer, I worked two evening shifts per week in the small Emergency Room of that faith-based community hospital. On a Friday night that hadn't been as busy as usual, a car sped down the driveway and stopped, engine running, outside the loading dock doors, and two young men ran in, covered in blood.

"You've got to help us!" they cried. "Our friend has been stabbed!"

We ran out to the car and saw the young man propped up in the back seat by a terrified third young man. The victim, extremely pale, wasn't moving. Like his friends, he was covered in blood as more oozed slowly from a wound in his left chest.

"There was a fight on the beach!" they all tried to explain. "Someone stabbed him! With this!" the third young man sobbed, holding out a long, thin-bladed knife.

The physician, ED orderly, and I looked at each other in shock, realizing there was no hope of saving that young man. He had bled out when his friends pulled the knife from the wound. They hadn't known not to remove an impaled object from a potentially lethal injury.

We managed to get him out of the car, onto a stretcher, and into the ED exam room until the police in Port Hueneme, where the incident had occurred, could begin the investigation. In those summer months of 1964, CPR was still not universally practiced, and there was no trauma center near where the stabbing had occurred. No one could have saved him at that time and in that place, but that didn't make us feel any better. Losing any patient, especially one so young, hurt all of us.

That same summer, on the July 4th weekend, I was again on evening shift duty in the ED. My husband was at home with our three-month-old baby, which was just as well since that shift lasted far longer than scheduled, and I wouldn't be home until well after 2 a.m.

Fairly early that evening, we were notified to expect a middle-aged man, badly burned in a boat explosion at the marina. Having neither trauma center nor Burn Unit, we prepared to admit him with a great deal of trepidation about the outcome. Our little Emergency Department was equipped with just the basics. We would stabilize him, then transport him to a burn center out of our own Ventura County. Those were the early days of pre-hospital care, with only private ambulance companies available for transport. Trauma care training for the paramedics and emergency medical technicians hadn't yet become part of Emergency care, and advanced cardiac life support was still in its infancy.

Normally, an ED physician would accompany a severely injured patient by land transport, but we had only one physician on duty that night. I was delegated to go with the patient in the ambulance and tend to him while the crew navigated and drove us to the Burn Center at the University of California Los Angeles Medical Center in downtown Los Angeles.

My patient had been thrown into the engine when his boat exploded, causing deep lacerations to his chest wall and arms already charred by his third and fourth-degree burns. Fully awake throughout his ordeal, his airway had been partially compromised by the fire, but he wasn't intubated, could talk to me, and was doing well on high flow oxygen. "I'm sorry to be so much work for you," he told me time after time as I held his one unburned hand and offered what comfort I could. The burns were extensive, nerve endings destroyed. I could at least offer emotional support to this man who faced a lengthy and painful recovery, if he managed to survive.

"You're not so much work for me," I reassured him. "And I get to hold your hand all the way to Los Angeles!"

The cardiac monitor indicated a rapid heart rate associated with his injuries, but he'd been healthy and active until this accident and remained stable all the way to downtown Los Angeles, well over a hundred miles to the south. I ran intravenous fluids as rapidly as possible through his two antecubital intravenous lines to maintain hydration and tried to keep calm and competent for this man who, for the entire trip, continued apologizing.

Los Angeles County General Hospital had one of the nursing schools I considered applying to years before. It was widely recognized for its Burn Unit, so I knew that this remarkable man, who had never complained, would be treated as expeditiously and comprehensively as possible. He was still alive and stable when we arrived, but I worried about his outcome all the way back to Oxnard that night and for the next few days until I learned, sadly, that he had died in the Burn Unit, overwhelmed by the sepsis that so often killed burn victims.

For weeks, I brooded about that young man stabbed to death and the burned man who had tried so hard to stay alive. I anguished over how helpless I'd felt at their outcomes but would soon be reminded that other forces were out there that would test me in my chosen profession. One day after that ambulance trip to Los Angeles, David told me he didn't want to hear any more about my patients or my worries about them, which increased the tension between us at home. I had no family there, and no close friend yet in Oxnard to talk to, so for those first months at St. John's, I felt unaccountably alone.

The Emergency physician who had been on duty both nights was one of the best I met in California. But like Florence Nightingale, who often clashed with arrogant and officious doctors in her lengthy career, I locked horns with a few of the same during mine. One of the most annoying was the one I met in that first nursing position in California, and it all started with a phone call. The Director of Nursing, unwilling to buck a member of the medical staff, had agreed with his demand to remove me from the ED when I dared to question a medication order and refused to medicate one of his patients, already in several times that week for narcotic injections for his chronic abdominal pain. The physician had always provided it, and when he was not on site in the ED, he would call in his standard orders for Demerol, one of the most frequently ordered and most addictive narcotics provided to patients in the1960s.

Since accepting telephone orders from physicians was standard nursing practice, and I knew that the patient was in constant pain, the issue was not in carrying out the order but in who had called it in. "Who did you say this is?" I asked when an unfamiliar voice answered the phone when I called the physician at home. He had left the ED an hour earlier for a family emergency. No other physician was on duty that night, and I'd called this one at home often in the few months that I worked there.

When there was no answer, just dead silence, I asked again, "Who is this?"

Still silence, and then, "My dad said to give the patient fifty milligrams of Demerol. It's what he always gets."

I was speechless. This had never happened to me before, and I was not about to accept a telephone order for a narcotic from his teenaged son. I refused to accept it and asked to speak with the physician. When he finally came on the line, and I explained that orders for narcotics from his teenage son were not covered by my nursing license, he lost his temper.

"Who the hell do you think you are? Do you know who I am? Your superior, that's who I am. You're incompetent, and I demand to speak to your supervisor!"

"Go ahead and call her," I said. "Your patient has waited too long already for this medication. I'll be happy to give it if you provide the order." Still furious, he hung up on me, and the patient had another medication delay until the Nursing Supervisor could persuade that ED physician to provide the order.

That was my last shift in the Emergency Department, and there was no recourse. In those days, in the early 1960s, physicians could and often did dismiss nurses for whatever reasons they chose. This one had been unprofessional to have his son call in the order, and my nursing license would have been in jeopardy if I'd acted on it. The potential for losing my license couldn't have mattered less to him. What motivated him was the power he could exercise over Nursing Administration. Because he knew he had it, he didn't hesitate to use it.

I didn't tell David about it for two reasons: he had warned me not to tell him about my patient care concerns, and I knew he would have allied himself with this ED physician, whom he had admired since beginning his position in the Pharmacy in June. When it came to hospital politics, a physician was a stronger ally for a pharmacist than a nurse, even if the pharmacist and the nurse were married to each other. David and I never discussed it, but my nursing colleagues agreed that I had done the right thing, and even the Pharmacy Director admitted that the physician had been wrong.

Sometimes, things seem to happen for a reason. I liked my new assignment to the Medical and Surgical units where I'd spent so much time at Bellevue, and then, a few months later, my next assignment, to the fledgling Intensive Care Unit, was a perfect fit. The cardiologist who had instituted the cardiac monitoring classes and set the criteria for Coronary Care and Intensive Care admissions couldn't have been more supportive of the nursing staff. He was one of several physicians in that small community hospital in Ventura County who contributed so much to my professional growth. I never forgot his early encouragement and support.

During my six years at St. John's, I learned cardiac care, intensive care, and medical and surgical care in all the major subspecialties. We had Michael, our second child, in 1965, and I worked part-time before and after his birth, as well. In February 1967, we had Tracy, our third child, and I returned to my part-time staff position several months later. I had to take a leave of absence in the fourth month of that pregnancy due to premature rupture of my amniotic membranes. It was a miracle that the pregnancy continued, no sepsis occurred, and I delivered a healthy eight-and-a-half-pound baby girl.

In the seven years since our marriage, we had moved four times, starting from our apartment in Lakewood, Washington, to our motel in Oxnard, California, where we stayed while David looked for a job. Our first home in California was the small apartment near the hospital where we got our first jobs; the second was the larger one we rented when we had our second child; and the third was the brand-new home we bought before our third child arrived. We had three beautiful children and were busy with all the activities and commitments experienced by young families in the 1960s. We had no idea how radically our lives were about to change as we entered the 1970s.

Chapter Six

THE SURPRISING SEVENTIES

AS I APPROACHED thirty, I felt I needed more challenges. My involvement in a social sorority kept me busy in a non-professional capacity, and my continued interest in the evolving specialty of nephrology led me to founding the Ventura County chapter of the Southern California Kidney Foundation. I'd taken all the educational courses offered at St. John's, had been certified and re-certified in Basic and Advanced Cardiac Life Support, and was looking for more professional experience than could be found at the hospital in Oxnard.

I also felt I needed more than nursing to round out a busy life as wife and mother. I didn't know what that was, but my life as I'd lived it so far was about to change, and I would soon learn how very painful that change would be.

County General was the hospital that would provide me with a wider variety of those challenges. Located in Ventura, a coastal city twenty miles to the north and just south of Santa Barbara, it was more up-to-date and served a greater patient population. I was thrilled that my application had been accepted and looked forward to starting in January 1970, but fate had something else in mind for me.

Just after the New Year, my husband, an avid skier who by now would rather be out on the slopes and nowhere near the pharmacy at St. John's, invited me to go with him on his next trip to the mountains.

"It's just for the day," he insisted. "Sometimes I just need to get away, and this will be a perfect time for me to take you skiing."

We hired a babysitter to care for our children, ages three, four, and five, and took off for what should have been a relaxing day for both of us. It was my first time on skis, and just as I started getting the hang of it, I fell. Badly. It was at the end of the day. I was heading down to the lodge to turn in my skis after an impressive run—my first one that day—when wham! My left knee buckled, my left ski slid sideways, and the binding refused to release. I landed in a tangled heap, couldn't get up, and just knew I'd broken my left knee. I glanced around at all the other skiers looking so concerned for me and laughed at my own embarrassment. It was either that or burst into tears, and I was absolutely not going to do that. "Damn! I was hoping nobody would notice!" I said, smiling through the pain. I was beyond embarrassed to be hauled off the bunny slope in one of those rescue sleds, but laughing at myself made it much easier.

I knew David was disappointed with me. Both of us unhappy at how the day ended, we made it safely home with my leg in a makeshift splint, and I ended up the next day at St. John's for orthopedic surgery.

After two days, my orthopedist applied a cast from ankle to thigh, and I put aside my plans for the new job at Ventura County General. Keeping up on crutches with three kiddies under six and unable to drive my car became more painful than the injury itself. David kept right on skiing. I was hoping he would help more at home, but skiing during his days off had become a controlling passion. I didn't like it, but I didn't dwell on it. Instead, I spent more quality time with Laura, Michael, and Tracy and kept them busy at home by keeping their rooms clean, helping with the laundry, and assisting me with meal planning and cooking. "You all take turns picking what you want for dinner, and then you can help me fix it," I told them. That was a big hit but meant a lot of hot dogs, hamburgers, and pizza, as well as the more nourishing meals I cooked for all of us.

During those six weeks from early January through mid-February while the fracture healed and I completed the physical therapy program, I saved my sanity by again applying for the position at Ventura County General. Human Resources said they would hold it for me, so that was no longer a worry. Since I couldn't yet drive to the library, I re-read my favorite books and wrote long letters to my parents and my sister, Carroll. In my quiet time, I reminisced about my orientation into the Army at Fort Sam Houston seven years before, and, in February, I decided to try writing a book about it.

That book became *Army Daze,* the fiction-based-on-fact account of my short-lived career in the Army Nurse Corps. I did it in longhand, then typed it laboriously on my portable typewriter while my kiddies napped or slept. I didn't know what I would do with it when I finished, but writing it was a labor of love and brought back some happy memories.

David continued working at the job he hated and went skiing whenever he had a day off. I didn't understand why he had to spend so much of our income on ski equipment and lift tickets but kept those questions to myself. By 1970, still early in our marriage, I'd learned to simply accept whatever concerned me, but it was taking its toll. I resented that his happiness came first while mine and that of our three young children came second.

I began the nursing position at Ventura County General in April 1970, and for six months I happily floated from floor to floor, to Intensive Care and to the Medical-Surgical services, admitting and caring for my own patients as well as assisting my overworked colleagues during our busy 3 p.m. to 11 p.m. shifts. Those shifts provided opportunities to enhance my nursing skills, and I still enjoyed those professional challenges. Everything was finally going well until October, when my husband unexpectedly decided to resign his position as pharmacist at St. John's.

"You did what?" I asked when he told me he was leaving a respected position at St. John's to take one in retail pharmacy, which he'd never even considered. "And to go where?"

"Bishop. There was an opening and—"

"And?" There had to be something else.

"It's close to Mammoth," he confessed, "and I'll be able to ski as much as possible on my days off." Skiing. He wanted more skiing, as though all that he'd been doing the past winter wasn't enough.

"And what about the rest of us?" I demanded. "Two of our kids are in school. I have a job I love. We have a beautiful home, and you want us to leave all that so you can go skiing?"

In 1970, wives still changed their lives at their husbands' whims to keep the peace. It was what my mother had done with the moves my father had made in their long marriage, and I didn't really have a choice.

David had already accepted a position as a retail pharmacist and would be moving us to the high desert city of Bishop, California. Convinced this move would place him in a position more to his liking than the one at St. John's Hospital and satisfy his need to ski as often as possible, he insisted we rent out our home in Oxnard and sell it once the position in Bishop became permanent.

Reluctantly, I went along with the plan. I found renters for our house, transferred Laura and Michael's academic records to the school in Bishop, packed everything we owned to load into the rental truck, and worked my last shift at Ventura General. We left Oxnard the last week in October, and, once we arrived in Bishop, I repainted and re-decorated the house we rented there. Laura and Michael liked their new school, and Tracy made some new friends her own age.

By the third week in November, we'd all somehow survived that huge upheaval in our lives, and I was preparing to apply for a nursing position at the community hospital in Bishop when the bottom fell out of our lives once again. When David refused to follow his employer's demands to forge state of California medication reimbursement forms, he lost his retail pharmacist position.

"You did the right thing," I said. "I'm proud of you for doing it, but what are we going to do now?"

"I don't know, but we can't stay here. I'll talk to my brother, Bill. Maybe he'll know someone in Sacramento who knows someone who needs a pharmacist."

There was no apology for what he'd already put us through with the move to Bishop or for what faced us now. I knew my recriminations wouldn't help, so I held them in, did my best to keep things positive for the kids and to make the trip to Sacramento seem like an adventure, but I was shaking inside.

We'd have to leave the home we'd rented in Bishop. David had no job, I hadn't yet applied for one in Bishop, and two of our children had already started school there. With no solid plans, we packed up our possessions, moved out of the rental home, and that Thanksgiving Day, 1970, left for Sacramento, where he hoped to secure another position in retail pharmacy. It was the lowest point in our young marriage. I was unhappy and knew it was time to set some of my own goals if we had any chance of saving it.

By the end of November, we'd settled in Fair Oaks, a suburb north of Sacramento. David had finally found a position in retail pharmacy in Citrus Heights, our son and older daughter started school once again, and I made our rental home, the second in two months, more habitable for all of us.

The year 1970 rolled into 1971. There were no nursing positions open the first few months of that new year. I had enrolled in the local community college and taken the English IA class required to apply for the two-year Associate in Arts degree before we left for Bishop. Now, with no nursing jobs available, I thought about going back to school with the goal of eventually earning a degree in Speech Pathology and Audiology. My husband refused to consider it.

"You're just a nurse," he snapped, "and a wife and mother. You're not a college student. You have me and three kids to think about. Forget going back to school!"

That was the last straw, especially after the debacle of the move to Bishop. I was absolutely furious, and, for the first time in our marriage,

I let him know it. "Nobody is *just* anything, and I am definitely not just a nurse. Every minute of every day, I know that I'm your wife and the mother of our children. I know I'm damned lucky to have all of you in my life, but don't you dare tell me that my going to school will destroy all that!"

I was thirty years old, and I'd grown in so many ways since our marriage in 1963. I knew there was more I could learn, that the one college English class I had taken had helped to open up a world of possibilities that could enhance all our lives. In those seven years, I'd had our three children, plus two miscarriages, in pretty rapid succession. I'd totally committed myself to that marriage and to our family, but, at thirty, I wanted something more for myself.

Unable to convince David I could handle school while devoted to him and Laura, Michael, and Tracy, and still on hold for any available nursing positions, I was desperate to find something besides childcare and humoring an increasingly unhappy husband. A week after I told David how I felt, I found a job that would provide a challenge without placing any stress on the family.

The Sacramento County School System had advertised for a registered nurse to teach a nursing aide course on Monday evenings at Hiram Johnson High School. I'd been terrified of public speaking since I was a teenager and, until then, avoided all opportunities to conquer that fear, but this was an opportunity I couldn't miss. I applied for the position and, to my amazement, got the job. All I had to do was conquer that old terror of public speaking. It helped that I'd be teaching something I knew inside out. The students could learn from me about competent and compassionate patient care, and this course would help them to provide it.

I absolutely loved it. Teaching younger and older adults from varied backgrounds the basics of patient care offered the challenges I needed and rewards I never expected. From the earliest days of our marriage, my husband had been clear that his education as a pharmacist was far superior to mine. Now, he was forced to see me in a different light.

He didn't like it, but he dropped his objection to my taking classes at American River, the community college near our home in Fair Oaks.

"So, you're not just a damned nurse after all!" he told me the evening I finished teaching the course, his anger barely controlled. "But you still have me and three kids to take care of, and what are you going to do when you start school?"

"I'll get a babysitter for them on the two days that I have classes. They think it's great that their mom will be going to school and that they'll have their favorite babysitter when I'm not there. You know, you might want to check out extension classes toward your own degree." I refused to let him ruin this for me and hoped that he would see that I still supported him in his career.

David liked retail pharmacy even less than his clinical pharmacist position in Oxnard. He had graduated from pharmacy school at the University of the Pacific and also regretted not staying for a fifth year to earn the Doctor of Pharmacy degree. The successes that his classmates had achieved in the years since graduation had become another source of stress for him, and drinks after work with his current employer became a daily occurrence. While those drinks made the hated job and his frustrating life more bearable for him, it soon became another source of stress on our already fragile marriage.

Succeeding in that part-time teaching position changed me. It gave me confidence and the knowledge that I could someday enhance my nursing career or change my professional focus entirely. When I finished teaching the nursing aide course, I secured a part-time position in the Emergency Department of a local community hospital, then completed the courses required for entrance into Sacramento State University the following year.

I'd always assumed the GI Bill was available only to male veterans. I applied anyway and was delighted to learn that my time in service qualified me for thirty-six units of educational benefits, which would help defray costs for my tuition and childcare. David and our three children were included in the monthly allotments, and now our household budget wouldn't be affected by my tuition and childcare costs.

"So, you've got it all figured out," he said when I told him about the GI Bill. "Good for you! Go on! Get your damned degree. I don't care!"

David was now at a standstill in his career and stuck in a profession he hated, while I was someone entirely new, more independent, and no longer willing to accept how thoroughly he tried to control me. He once loved the young woman I had been, the New York Army Nurse who had intrigued him when we met in Texas. And I'd loved that tall and tan California man who'd seemed so right for me. What had happened to us? I didn't know how to fix it, and he didn't seem to want to, so we went on, each of us stubbornly committed to the marriage that we had so hopefully entered almost ten years before.

Although it wasn't easy, work and school schedules were planned around our children's school schedules and David's work assignments. Our children thrived, and I felt fulfilled, but my husband, resentful that I could juggle all those responsibilities, became more distant and demeaning. The drinking didn't make things easier.

Nursing would always be my primary career, but I loved going back to school and meeting challenges so different from those I'd met in three years at Bellevue. A liberal arts education was a gift that could enhance my professional pursuits, and I intended to make the most of it. I still worked per diem in our local hospital ED and suspected, by then, that I'd probably need to keep those nursing skills current if I ever became the primary support for our children.

In that small but busy ED, I continued to hone patient care skills and adapt to more changes in nursing, and, through the end of 1972, I balanced home, family, school, and work with no encouragement or support from David. He did enroll in evening courses to apply to a graduate degree in Business Administration, but, unable to maintain a C average, he gave up in frustration.

In the fall of 1972, I transferred to Sacramento State University to study Speech Pathology and Audiology. Unfortunately, the program was designed for speech and hearing programs in grade schools and high schools, not the neurologically impaired patients I had hoped to treat. Already in my junior year, I decided to change majors.

Nursing would have been the logical choice, but the state of California wouldn't accept diploma nursing school courses for its bachelor's in nursing degree. Although the majority of the diploma program at Bellevue had been taught by highly qualified instructors from New York University, none of my education there, one of the most prestigious nursing schools in the country, had been accepted. I was told I'd need to challenge all the Bellevue courses with no guarantee of acceptance into the program at Sacramento State University. In addition, the Veterans Administration wouldn't authorize support for the newly required courses I'd already successfully completed at Bellevue, so I decided to complete my degree in English and continue on for the Master's in Creative Writing.

Again, my classes were all arranged around my children's schedules, and their after-school activities were geared to the availability of babysitters who became part of our everyday lives. The children knew how hard I worked at my studies, and they worked equally hard at theirs. I remember the evenings we sat around the kitchen table after dinner, talking about our day while we did our homework and David watched television by himself. Laura, Michael, and Tracy knew there was tension between the two of us and made the best of it. The only unhappy member of our family was their father, still regretting that decision he'd made to leave the clinical pharmacist position at St. John's for the one that ended so badly in Bishop. Bitterly resentful, he made home life for all of us miserable.

At thirty-three, I completed the Bachelor of Arts in English and ten months later received my Master of Arts in Creative Writing. My GI Bill benefits had officially ended in March but had been extended by the Veterans Administration through the completion of the Master of Arts degree that August.

All along, nursing was part of that busy life, working per diem in the ED in that small community hospital and Critical Care in other facilities in the Sacramento area. In the fall of 1975, that part of my life expanded once again. Based on that earlier course for the nursing aide students at Hiram Johnson High School and my current emergency and critical care experience, I applied for and accepted a substitute clinical instructor position for the Associate Degree Nursing Program at Sacramento City College. Because I'd earned the master's degree in a non-nursing specialty, the appointment covered only one semester, so while I waited to begin that new semester in January, I completed the requirements for the Community College Instructor credential.

I was assigned to fourth semester students in the Associate in Science degree in Nursing program, which included in-class instruction in Nursing Leadership and Critical Care with on-site mentoring of the students at the County Hospital in Sacramento. This was another challenge I couldn't ignore. As my love for teaching grew, David became more resentful and bitter. Despite the fact that I was working normal hours, had every weekend free, and now contributed a much better paycheck to our joint account, he refused to recognize my contribution to our family.

Eventually what would become the University of California, Davis, Medical Center, County Hospital/Sacramento Medical Center was the on-site location for nursing students assigned to patients in the various critical care areas in the hospital, including Coronary Care, Medical Intensive Care, Neurological Intensive Care, Surgical Intensive Care, and Burn Unit.

In the mid 1970s, patient care in Sacramento was still evolving. More materials were disposable, technology was rapidly advancing, and the patients were cared for by medical students, interns, residents, and attending physicians associated with the University of California, Davis, Medical School. A sizable portion of the patient population, the destitute and homeless, reminded me of patients I had cared for at Bellevue, and students were fortunate to experience a wide variety of nursing care opportunities not usually seen in community hospitals.

The six months from January through June were exciting and much more intense than I had expected. On-site at the medical center, I was in my element and did my best to instill in the students what I had learned about competent and compassionate patient care at Bellevue. But at the college campus in Sacramento, life as an instructor was often unsettling. As the youngest instructor and not a permanent member of the faculty, I encountered challenges not faced by long-term instructors. I didn't have an extensive background in education, and I'd gone outside nursing to earn my degrees in an entirely different discipline, which made some colleagues question my suitability to teach nursing. Most faculty members hadn't provided hands-on care to patients in years, and many hadn't kept current with the ever evolving technology. This particular class, due to graduate in June, had just survived an arduous third semester with an instructor who had been especially critical. I encouraged and supported them when their prior instructor had not made their last semester more than just bearable.

"You made this last semester our best," they told me after our final class together. "You helped us believe we belong in nursing, just as we know you do, and helped us understand how important kindness and compassion are to patient care. We'd love to have you be our commencement speaker."

By then, the summer of 1975, the stresses on an increasingly unhappy marriage had done their damage. Already resenting the completion of my degrees in English and creative writing, the success of the teaching role that had just ended, and the career successes of his friends and his former classmates after graduation from University of the Pacific, my husband made our life together impossible.

"You're just too damned perfect!" he told me on my last day as a substitute instructor, when I told the children after dinner about speaking at the school of nursing graduation.

"I know I'm not. But if I failed at this job and all the others I've tried since we left Bishop, you'd complain about that too!" I tried my best not to cry because he had started this latest altercation in front of our children, and I had to stay strong for them.

Nothing I did pleased David. The continued stress also affected our children, and five years after the disastrous move to Bishop, I seriously considered divorce. I wasn't sure it was the best option for all of us, but I knew that I had to do something to find the way back to the confident and hopeful young woman I had once been in the early days of our marriage.

Chapter Seven

ON MY OWN AGAIN

BECAUSE OF THE EXPERIENCE I acquired during all those months filling the temporary teaching position at City College, I applied for and was accepted as the Educator for the new Department of Critical Care at Sacramento Medical Center.

When I told David about this new position, he said, "It's just one more way to show me up. Go ahead and take it. I don't care what you do!" Embittered by his own failures, this latest tirade signaled the end for me.

"That's it. I'm done. You can't make up your mind if I'm 'too perfect' or too impossible to live with. You're so miserable you can't even see how hard you've been on all of us!"

Finally in a full-time position at a salary that would support me and our children, I could now ask for a divorce. All those years of study and preparation had been an essential step in ending a marriage that had been, at the end, a failure, and that bitter "I don't care what you do!" had made my decision inevitable.

If we'd been stronger and committed to our marriage, it might have survived. We'd been virtual strangers, too young and too naïve when we met. Our backgrounds and upbringing had been too diverse, and we hadn't been able to adapt to all the major stressors in our lives. More positive than my husband, I'd been better able to cope with most of them and move forward. Able to focus only on the successes of all his college classmates, he couldn't see a way to achieve his own success and bitterly resented mine. Finally, I was no longer "just the nurse" that he had designated me, and he had come to hate me for it.

The position at Sacramento Medical Center became another opportunity to grow. As Critical Care Educator, I replaced the colleague who'd recently retired, and I now worked with fellow educators in Medical, Surgical, Women and Children, and the Clinics. Our offices were located in the two-storied stucco and red-tile-roofed building to the right of the hospital property facing the parking lot and major city streets. We worked on the first floor in individual cubicles and had access to the main hospital by way of the side and front doors directly across the parking lot. All of us arranged and taught classes in our specialties and worked closely with each other in mutual support of our programs. At thirty-five, I was younger than Rina, the Medical and Surgical educator, the same age as Sherry, the educator for all the Clinics, and a little older than Joelle, the Women and Children Services educator.

My province was the critical care areas on the third, fourth, and fifth floors of the hospital comprising Medical Intensive Care, Coronary Care, Neurological Intensive Care, Burn Unit, and Surgical Intensive Care. At that time, from 1976 to 1979, Critical Care was still evolving, and we were all learning. Advances had been made in cardiac surgical techniques, pulmonary medicine, neurological monitoring, and care of septic burn patients. There were registered nurses far more adept and experienced than I was in the ever changing technologies and working with all the biomedical equipment that became increasingly complex. My role was to develop and provide courses for them and support all the critical care staff in providing access to what they were required to know for their own units.

From the beginning, I had more goals in mind than just learning the new technology, and, fortunately, I'd had the time and the resources to achieve them. I enjoyed providing educational support to the

Critical Care staff in all the units, but I also hoped to expand the horizons of those nurses in the medical-surgical units and Emergency Department who hoped to transfer to Critical Care.

By the summer of 1979, I had accomplished what I'd set out to do when I'd accepted the position. Before I left to take on different and more intense challenges in a community hospital north of Sacramento, I had designed and coordinated the first Critical Care Orientation Program for all registered nursing staff in Emergency, Critical Care, and Medical-Surgical services who wished to initiate or update their critical care skills. A complex multi-level project, it was the first of its kind at the Medical Center and the model for the first community-based critical care orientation course in the greater Sacramento area.

On a personal level, I'd learned that being a single parent was far from easy with three children in their teens and all of them rebellious. My son had chosen to live with his father, and my two daughters and I settled for apartment living in Citrus Heights, a busy suburb north of Sacramento. I kept in touch with Michael by phone when I could find time during my hectic schedule. Laura and Tracy, going through their own changes as teenagers, weren't happy that I worked so hard but were relieved that the anger and unhappiness during the last years with their father had ended. They had their own friends, got along well enough as sisters, and neither of them liked the men I dated.

I'd met quite a few of them in those years from age thirty-five to thirty-nine, and most were choices I'd come to regret. I probably would have made similar choices in my twenties if I hadn't married. But I'd grown up, started a new life, and become a person in my own right. Mistakes were bound to happen.

I still had a lot to learn, and infatuation followed infatuation. Just about all were with Mr. Wrongs, but one with Jay, a quirky business-man from San Francisco, led to an unexpected fascination with flying. A few years younger than I, he had his own plane and would fly up from the Bay area on weekends in his Cessna and take me on flights all over northern California. Because of Jay, I not only overcame a life-long distrust of airplanes, but I also actually learned how to fly them. Within months of our meeting, I'd taken and passed the required course in Ground School and taken my first flight in a Piper at the airport in Cameron Park.

After that, entranced, I enrolled for my flight lessons at the Executive Airport in Sacramento and flew those tiny little Pipers around the greater Sacramento metro area with Bruce, my extremely patient instructor. After just under thirty hours, we flew together out to Woodland one afternoon, landed the Piper Cub at the Yolo County Airport, and he turned the controls over to me. "It's time," he told me. "You're ready."

Terrified but determined to do this, I took off on my first solo from that 6,000-foot-long runway, flew up to 3,000 feet, cruised over the countryside south of Sacramento, then made it back to the airport for a perfect ten-point landing. To this day, that has been the most exciting, most intense, most terrifying experience I've ever had. Heart still racing, hot tears streaking my face, I climbed out of the plane and ran over to hug Bruce. "Thank you! You made that possible, and I'll never forget it!"

He taught me everything I would need to know during those weeks that he'd been my instructor. The worst lesson had been putting the plane into a steep climb, causing it to stall, and then showing me how to save myself and the plane when it went into a potentially fatal spin. If the plane lost lift and thrust, it would lose power and go down. Learning how not to panic and how to correct the spin could save my life and those of potential passengers.

For the next few weeks, I went on to finish my solo flights over Sacramento, keying in the radio in-flight and avoiding all the air traffic obstacles involving the multitudes of civilian and military flights over and around the greater metropolitan area. I had one moment of pure terror early one afternoon on my own. Flying over south Sacramento, experiencing the absolute joy of doing something I'd never dreamed possible, I heard a loud bang outside the plane, looked up and saw that the lock holding the hatch door above my head had opened and the door was doing its best to fly open. My heart thudded in my chest and my hands on the controls turned to ice. My abdominal muscles clenched, and I almost forget to breathe.

"What do I do now?" I asked, with nobody there to hear me. This was one problem Bruce had never covered in our many flights together. "I'm much too young to die!" I told myself. "The kids need me, and there's so much more I want to do." Not sure what would happen if that hatch actually flew open, I knew I had to do something, and I had to do it now.

Pilot error is often the major cause of small airplane accidents, so I calmed down and decided to head out to Woodland and to the Yolo County Airport where I'd flown my first solo. That 6,000-foot runway was long enough to land the Piper, relock the hatch, and head back to Executive Airport in Sacramento.

My heart was still thudding in my chest, but I willed my hands to stop shaking as I told Bruce about it when I landed. I wanted to be sure he knew about the latch and would see that the same thing didn't happen to another would-be pilot.

"You did exactly the right thing," he said. "Thank you for keeping your head and for getting yourself and your airplane back safely." We both knew the outcome could have been quite different.

The infatuation with the San Francisco pilot ended once I admitted to myself that the excitement of flying was what had held us together. He was funny and charming but not the right man for a single woman with three children. The adrenalin rush of our courtship couldn't last, and, in late summer1979, my solo flying ended as well. I had avoided disaster a time or two, had overcome my lifelong fear of flying, and was ready to take on the next challenge when I accepted a mid-level management position in the Roseville community hospital several miles north of where I lived in Citrus Heights.

I'd soon learn that political intrigues experienced during my past three years as an educator at Sacramento Medical Center had been a walk in the park compared to what faced me in Roseville.

Chapter Eight

INTO THE FIRE

THOSE PAST THREE years balancing the role of educator between Administration and Nursing hadn't been easy. We had worked under the aegis of Hospital Administration and Clinics, and Nursing Administration had bitterly resented it. Tensions had run high as Nursing Administration had continued to petition for our reassignment, but none of that prepared me at all for the firestorm of an administrative, medical, and nursing conflict awaiting me in that small district hospital north of Sacramento.

It was late summer 1979, seventeen years after my graduation from Bellevue. Designing and successfully delivering the comprehensive Critical Care Program at the Sacramento Medical Center had pushed me out of my comfort zone. I'd had no clear idea how to carry it out when I began, and no idea when I accepted the mid-level nursing management position in that community hospital in Roseville how I'd fill the shoes of the woman who had held it for more than a dozen years.

My responsibilities included Emergency, Coronary Care, and Intensive Care, the three most difficult to manage areas in the hospital, but I was determined to try. In the past few years, I'd worked quite a few per diem shifts there in all three units to keep my hands-on skills current while acting as Educator at the Medical Center and was not a total stranger to staff, but that didn't help me now.

When I accepted the role of Director, I wasn't told that the hospital was in the throes of a conflict that would have a far-reaching impact on all aspects of patient care. Three attending physicians, the department heads of Emergency, Obstetrics and Gynecology, and Surgery, had all challenged the authority of the Chief Executive Officer as well as the Chief Nursing Executive, and the fallout affected everyone. As healthcare had evolved during the past several decades, not only physicians and nurses but professional healthcare administrators now provided oversight of all medical center activities. The physicians at the hospital in Roseville hadn't accepted the Chief Executive Officer or the Chief Nursing Executive. Arriving in the middle of the conflict and allied with the Chief Nursing Executive, I was suspect. With ninety staff assigned to me, it was a tough time to hit the ground running and to quickly learn the role of a mid-level nursing manager.

Each of my three areas had strong leaders, so I decided not to micromanage any of them and offered only guidance and assistance when requested. Coronary Care and Intensive Care were no problem, but the Emergency Department was a different story. The Medical Director there had been furious when his own choice for nursing director in a department separate from all other nursing units in the hospital was rejected. An ex-Air Force physician with antiquated ideas about pre-hospital care, he resented the fact that not only was I not his choice for director, but I also dared to challenge his belief that paramedics and emergency medical technicians would never replace private ambulance personnel in this area of California.

"So, it's happening in Seattle and other cities," he sneered as he faced me down during a meeting with the Emergency Department staff. "That doesn't mean it will happen here or in any of the hospitals in Sacramento. And what the hell do you know about it? I'm a doctor, and you're just a damned know-it-all nurse!"

"I'm not just a damned know-it-all nurse, but I do know that change is inevitable. Healthcare is changing faster than anyone in the

1960s ever imagined. Pre-hospital care is changing right along with inpatient care, and so is nursing. In the past seventeen years, I've been a part of it, and there is definitely a change in pre-hospital care in Sacramento right now. I've seen it and worked with it. And you might be a physician, but you have no right to insult me or anyone else in this room!" I said as I pushed back my chair and left, probably the first person in years to have dared to tell him off.

This was the last year the nursing staff in the hospital would wear all white uniforms and the distinctive nursing caps of their individual schools of nursing. The Chief Nursing Executive's school of nursing had been Cook County in Chicago and mine was Bellevue in New York. She had formerly been in a religious order, and I'd been in the Army. I'd spent my early years in nursing in Southern California and, most recently, in Sacramento. Most of the staff, employed only at that facility for many years and with limited exposure to many new techniques and technologies, saw us as outsiders. Like the antagonistic Emergency Medical Director, they didn't accept us.

By late 1979, I was still there, still struggling, but the Chief Nursing Executive had now resigned and left the area. Our Administrator-CEO was barely hanging on as challenges to his authority continued. I had retained Directorship in Intensive Care but had stepped down from my roles in Coronary Care and Emergency. The Coronary Care nurses wanted one of their own staff to be Director, which was fine with me, and major changes had occurred in the Emergency Department that eliminated my role there.

The favored staff member there was promoted to Director, as her Medical Director and mentor demanded, and the Emergency Department was no longer under the direction of Nursing Administration. Ironically, that nurse who had waited so long for her promotion to Director resigned only months later when her affair with a married hospital executive went public. His marriage ended, and they promptly left for Japan. Both the Emergency Medical Director and his staff remained silent about her defection and continued to wage war against the CEO. I was thankful to no longer be a part of it.

I had finally met John, the Mr. Right who would become my second husband. A member of the hospital engineering staff, he had been supportive of me from the beginning and continued to be as I faced new problems in my remaining unit, Intensive Care, during the fall of 1979 and spring of 1980. John had come into the Emergency Department one day during my orientation there to check on a blanket warmer that had suddenly shut down. A cheerful man about my age with dark hair and laughing eyes, he'd joked with the nurses as he showed them how to reset it and smiled shyly at me as he left. To me, he'd seemed down-to-earth and friendly and had an accent straight out of New York. "Where's he from?" I asked Marge, the charge nurse. "I'd know that accent anywhere!"

"Staten Island, I think. He's been here for about ten years. Everyone loves John. He's a great guy, and a single dad with three kids."

I liked him that first day and even more a week or so later when he followed me into the office shared by the nursing supervisors and unit directors and asked me in front of everyone, "Will you go out to dinner with me if I ask you?"

Instantly charmed, I'd laughed and said, "So ask me!"

In sharing memories of our childhoods in and around New York City, we became friends, and in sharing the trials of parenting six growing children, we became a couple. It wasn't an easy time for either of us, survivors of unhappy marriages and disasters we'd endured as singles, but we both wanted stability and a future together. We were married in the summer of 1980, and he was there for me through all the problems at work during the months to come.

Uneasy about the challenges to Administration by the medical staff and not certain where their loyalties should lie, my own staff started challenging my role as well. Although I offered to work in the unit as a staff member when we were short-handed, the role of director became an object of constant criticism by some of the staff nurses assigned there from various nursing agencies. Some complained about their schedules; others complained about their coworkers. It became a constant balancing act trying to keep the peace while encouraging the staff to provide excellent patient care.

In the spring of 1981, those problems intensified. Overriding my concerns, the Acting Director and Assistant Director of Nursing insisted I hire two nurses whose applications I had not approved. Both had problems with authority in prior positions and didn't appear to be good fits for our facility. I had strong leaders in ICU and initially strong support, but the forced hiring of these two nurses divided the unit. Some of the staff liked them, and others thought that nursing administration had made a mistake in hiring them. Although I had always strongly supported my staff and worked those additional hours with them providing hands-on care, I knew I wouldn't stay there much longer.

A new nursing executive was hired that spring and, with her, new staff who changed the focus of nursing there for years to come. She supported them in their constant controversies and challenged me to do the same. Not much was known about her except that she'd taught in the nursing program at California State University and had achieved local recognition due to the nursing care plans that could be adapted in all areas of nursing care. We soon learned that she'd never been a chief nursing executive, that her rule was law, and that her decisions could never be questioned.

I learned that the hard way when, on the day it was scheduled to begin, she canceled an orientation program co-designed with the Education Department for new staff in ICU and CCU. It covered the basics of arrhythmias and nursing care and was modeled on the one I'd designed and presented at the Medical Center in Sacramento.

Margaretta Wyatt was a painfully thin woman in her forties, with straw-colored hair that always looked uncombed and intense, pale blue eyes in a heavily made-up face. She never looked pleased, had the raspy voice of a frequent smoker, and neither looked nor acted like a nursing executive. She had been antagonistic toward me since our first meeting and started this one with, "I don't need to tell you why the class is canceled, Barbara, and my decision is final."

All I felt was rage. The members of the Education department and I had worked hard to design that orientation program, and canceling it was a direct attack on me. She was the antithesis of the nursing director who had hired me and had most likely seen me as a threat to her authority.

"My decision is final too," I said as I got up to leave. "I know very well why you did it. I have no interest in anything else you will say or do, and no interest in working here with you any longer. My resignation will be on your desk when I leave today. Life is too short to fight battles that aren't worth winning."

I had just turned forty, was nineteen years post-graduation from Bellevue, and had no clear idea of where to go from there. I suspected it would take years to recover from the disaster that had been my first foray into nursing middle management, so I accepted another challenge, in an entirely different area of patient care.

Once again unaware of what I was getting myself into, I landed in the middle of another administrative/medical nightmare far more intense and painful than the one I'd just survived. I wondered, as I set out to make the best of yet another impossible situation, what it was about nursing that kept me going back for more.

Chapter Nine

TRANSPLANTS, DIALYSIS, AND THE WONDERFUL WORLD OF LITIGATION

DURING THE FIRST six years in California in the 1960s with David and our children, I became active in the Southern California Kidney Foundation. As cofounder of the new Ventura County chapter, I learned a great deal more about kidney disease than I had as a student at Bellevue, where dialysis was rarely done, patients survived on diets of Coke syrup and sugar-coated butter balls to spare their kidneys, and transplantation was still in its infancy. The cofounder, Al Whalen, had renal failure and was undergoing dialysis, and my good friend Denise and her mother were also facing renal failure and the need for dialysis.

When I left Oxnard in 1970 and moved to North Central California, I also lost that early involvement with the Kidney Foundation and those colleagues and friends fighting their own kidney failure. Ten years later, when I accepted the position as Transplant Coordinator at the University of California, Davis, Medical Center, I knew fate had led me back to that vital element of my life lost so long ago. Unfortunately, that April 1981, I had no premonition that fate had also led me into the next healthcare disaster.

The previous coordinator had resigned, the Physician's Assistant who had monitored the program since then also left, and no one was willing to say why or where he had gone. With no one to orient me to the Transplant program and no warning of the impending crisis, I started that first week with high hopes but no clue how to perform my duties. The transplant surgeon had inexplicably left Sacramento for a medical conference in Qatar, and I only learned about that when I received a cryptic message on my first day to place a long-distance call to him there.

"Just check the patient records in the office across from the dialysis unit," he told me. "The list of patients scheduled to attend the Transplant Clinic is in the file cabinet under Clinic. Notify all of them to attend and take their medical records with you on Thursday afternoon." The telephone reception from Qatar was patchy. I could just barely hear him say as he hung up, "And check with my secretary about your trip to Chicago on Friday."

Chicago? On Friday? Nothing had been said about it until now, and nothing had been said about the Transplant Clinic. I was left with checking the patient records of those still actively followed in the Clinic and preparing to meet them Thursday afternoon in one of the many temporary trailers to the right of the hospital. When I called his secretary about Chicago, she impatiently told me, "Yes. A national conference on Transplantation."

"He never told me."

Her voice softened. "I'm not surprised. I'm sure he neglected to tell you a lot of things."

Before I could ask her what she meant, she informed me that I would fly to the conference on Friday, but there was no one in Transplant Services to accompany me or to brief me on the conference itself. I'd never been to Chicago, but determined to learn as much as possible to prepare for my job, I flew there on Friday and attended all the sessions on Saturday in the large inner-city hotel that been booked for the conference.

It was there, at the end of that long day during a news break from the local television station, that I learned that the transplant program and all future renal transplant surgeries at University of California, Davis, Medical Center in Sacramento had been terminated. I had absolutely no idea what to do next.

With no one from the program to explain what had happened and no one to call at the Medical Center since it was a Saturday, I felt betrayed and absolutely furious. I was alone in Chicago, representing a program facing closure and potential litigations. Someone at the medical center should have informed me about the pending program closure before I accepted the transplant position. Dejected, I stayed in my room that night and left for O'Hare International Airport early on Sunday morning for the first flight home.

On Monday, I was in my office on the fifth floor, across the hall from the Dialysis Unit, when I learned that not only the Transplant program but also the Thoracic Surgery program had been abruptly canceled, and the Medical Center was now inundated by an avalanche of lawsuits. Once again, through sheer bad luck, I found myself in the wrong place at the wrong time. I had a job—or didn't—and wouldn't hear the full extent of the disaster until several days after I returned from Chicago.

I spent those next few days waiting to hear from someone in Hospital Administration about what remained of the position I'd so eagerly accepted. I organized the files of those patients still being followed and attended the Transplant Clinic that Thursday. But it was not until Friday, a week since the news of the program closure, that I would learn what was expected of me in the weeks—and what turned out to be months—that followed.

At that time, patients who had been transplanted or awaited transplants had five options for treatment of their ESRD—End-Stage Renal Disease. They could choose center-based hemodialysis; home-based hemodialysis or peritoneal dialysis; transplant; or no treatment at all, just eventual chronic kidney failure and death. Many transplanted patients who came under my care had already had home or center-based dialysis or previous transplants that had failed. The remainder of them were the few for whom transplant at our medical center was no longer an option until the transplant program resumed . . . if it did.

My new role was to follow the patients who'd had transplants and, to my disbelief, to take a full-time position, ten hours a day, in the Hemodialysis Unit on the fifth floor of the hospital. I would carry the beeper and respond to patient calls, as well as to calls to and from the two major transplant centers in San Francisco, arranging for transport of donated organs from patients who had died in our area and whose families had honored their final wishes to become kidney donors.

This was still early in my second marriage. I was grateful none of this would impact John at work since the medical center in Sacramento wasn't directly associated with his facility in Roseville. We were both still trying to keep the peace at home between his three children, Lori, John, and Kristen and my daughter, Laura; he didn't want additional problems. The burden fell on me to handle it. I managed, but it was an early indication that maybe he would not, could not, always be there for me.

I remained on call twenty-four hours a day with no remuneration, no official program, no Medical Director, and no end in sight. Hoping to do my best for those patients abandoned in the middle of an untenable situation, I took on another impossible role in a career that had been anything but conventional, and I was absolutely disconsolate.

I started my second week following the closure of the transplant program reporting to the hemodialysis unit just across the hall from the transplant office, where I kept patient records and made necessary calls regarding their status. From 8 a.m. until after 4 p.m., Monday through Friday, I spent my time prepping the dialysis machines, helping place the fifteen to twenty patients we saw every day onto and off the machines for their three-hour runs, then taking down the machines to terminal clean them with formaldehyde at the end of each shift. No one in authority took any notice of the potential overexposure to formaldehyde, a hazard that should have been addressed long before my own assignment there and one of the primary reasons I dreaded working in dialysis.

In those months that followed, I often asked myself why I didn't just leave, but I believed I needed to be there for those post-transplant patients, most of whose transplants failed and were now back on dialysis. I was the only one to follow their post-transplant status, maintain their records, and find help for them because that's what a transplant coordinator did. With or without an official program, and with all attention focused on the litigations, I was now the only one to do it. I was physically exhausted, rarely saw my husband, but was grateful that all of the six children in our blended family were, so far, finally learning to get along.

Depending upon the acuity of their chronic renal failure, these patients either did very well or very badly in dialysis, and I soon learned that the more fluid we removed, the worse they felt. For most of them, those three days each week they were required to spend in dialysis became extremely daunting, and as much as I dreaded all those days in the unit, I did learn my new role.

As I worked with them on the days that they dialyzed, I became very attached to those men and women, some of whom had already had their transplants, who had developed problems in their grafts, and who had ended up right back on dialysis. "You only have to call me or stop me here in the Unit if you have a problem where I can help you," I told them. "The transplant program may be on hold, but I'm still your coordinator, and I'm here for you. Before you leave today, I'll give you my card with the numbers where you can contact me."

Machines had never been my strong suit, but I was determined to learn my new role well enough to safely "crash and burn" (totally dry out) my fragile patients and to go down to the intensive care units with the portable machine to dialyze the critically ill patients there.

Those weeks turned into months, and like most of the staff in our busy medical center, I often heard rumors about the increasing numbers of lawsuits being filed against the Transplant and Thoracic Surgery Services. I remained busy with the dialysis schedule and the Thursday clinic but had begun accepting occasional assignments on weekend night shifts in ICUs in and around Sacramento to keep my nursing skills current.

Still on the beeper and on-call for transplant patient crises or arranging to send the donated kidneys to transplant centers in San Francisco, I came into conflict fairly often in the next few months with nursing administration at the Medical Center. Not under the aegis of the Director of Nursing, I occasionally could not be immediately available for transplant issues when I was called. I did handle them as soon as possible and never refused to go into the Medical Center to tackle on-site transplant problems when needed.

"You know," I told the latest supervisor who had complained when it took a few minutes for me to get back to her, "I do have a life. I work full-time in the Dialysis Unit, and sometimes I take an extra shift in ED or ICU in other hospitals. I always take these Transplant calls and never refuse to come in for transplant or donor issues. But I've never been thanked for doing it or paid for being on call twenty-four hours a day. So back off, and let me do what I came in here to do!"

That same supervisor had also taken it upon herself to make calls to families of possible organ donors with no actual background in transplant protocol and no skill at speaking with the grieving families she contacted.

Looking back now, when I mention that stressful time in my nursing life to colleagues, I remember my commitment to patients already transplanted and my hope that I would be asked to continue as Transplant Coordinator when the program resumed. The patients themselves, so many of whom developed problems with their donated kidneys, were the primary reason I stayed and why, while I didn't enjoy my assignment in the Hemodialysis Unit, I enjoyed my long hours with them.

Most of them dialyzed for three hours, three times a week, were extremely supportive to each other, and appreciated all we did for them. The nursing staff there were exceptional, worked under always stressful time requirements, and were most sympathetic to me, trying to make the best of a tough situation. I remember all of it, the frantic placing of patients onto the machines, taking them off in order to dialyze the next influx of waiting patients, and the hours spent taking down and terminal cleaning the machines with formaldehyde to prepare them for the next dialysis sessions.

I remember the patients who became dear to me as they struggled with end-stage renal failure, graft rejection, and a plethora of problems that threatened their survival. Benny, who hated dialysis, faithfully checked in for his sessions and arrived from the ED every Monday morning after relapsing into ketoacidosis every weekend. He stubbornly insisted that dialysis would save him no matter what he did after his three-hour sessions. Iraj, a patient who came from Iran several years before and then developed kidney failure in California, barely tolerated dialysis just to be strong enough to go back to his own country to fight in the Iran-Iraq war. He was determined to return despite no assurance he could continue his treatments there.

The one I remember most for her courage was Ruthie, a poorly controlled diabetic woman in her sixties whose transplant had failed. Back on dialysis, she soon developed mucormycosis, an aggressive fungus that thrived in some patients with high blood glucose levels. It began in her right orbit, then moved into the left, and, to save her, the surgeons had no choice but to remove both eyes. She was strong throughout, never complained, accepted what had happened to her, and continued with dialysis until she succumbed to the fungus several months later.

In early 1982, my professional life took another unexpected turn. By now proficient in hemodialysis and expert in all aspects of acute and chronic renal failure, I was offered a newly created position that would utilize my expertise in transplant, dialysis, and the writing skills I honed at California State University. Hospital Administration asked me to become a Legal Liaison to Risk Management. My new role was to assess and then explain to the attorneys assigned to the Transplant litigations what had happened to all those patients who had experienced complications, whose transplants had failed, or who had died after transplant surgery. Finally, I was able to take a vital role in an entirely unexplored area of nursing practice, and it opened a whole new world for me.

Chapter Ten

LEGAL LIAISON AND PAPER CHASERS

AS LEGAL LIAISON to Risk Management, I was on the move again. This time it was from the fifth floor in the main hospital building to a temporary structure across the parking lot from the two-story building where off-duty physicians and staff slept while on call.

At the University of California, Davis, Medical Center, moving was what we all did best. We stayed in our temporary building for the first six months of 1983, well past the day when Wendi, my first granddaughter, was born at Mather Air Force Base in Sacramento. In June, we moved back into the first-floor offices in the on-call building where I had begun as the Critical Care Educator eight years before.

We'd needed more space once the multiple litigations got underway. Not only were there lawsuits levied against the Transplant Program but Thoracic Surgery as well. From the first, the work was overwhelming but a welcome break from dialysis and all the transplant issues. By then, the requirement to carry the beeper and to follow all the previously transplanted patients, as well as to coordinate organ donations for the two San Francisco transplant centers, had ended. Although I knew the decision to assign another coordinator to the old program once it resumed was the logical one, I was disappointed not to have been chosen. I had already been working on litigations and caring for remaining survivors of prior surgeries. What was now needed was a totally neutral person to launch a new program.

Thankfully, Risk Management soon absorbed all my time and attention. The attorneys for the university employed us to assist in evaluating all the medical records in the Cardiology, Thoracic Surgery, Nephrology and Transplant Programs, and a substantial number of cases in all three areas came under investigation.

A registered nurse who had been clinical coordinator of the Thoracic Surgery program became the primary liaison for those cases. I became the primary liaison for all the transplant cases due to my assignments to the suspended Transplant Program and dialysis for the past year and a half. Eventually, I was joined by two other registered nurses to assist with those cases and all others that came into the Risk Management department.

My primary role was to develop the assessment tool for evaluating the medical records of those patients or families who had filed lawsuits against the Transplant Program. Those were the days before the advent of electronic medical records, and special rooms designated for all the paper records were set aside for those of us who evaluated them. The work was arduous and time-consuming. Most records covered multiple admissions and were seldom limited to one volume; many of the records had been misfiled or gone missing.

Incredibly, it became apparent that physicians named in the litigations had taken the charts from the Medical Records department and never returned them. One of the physicians, a urologist who had accused fellow physicians in both Nephrology and Transplant Surgery of negligence and then initiated the legal actions, was required to return all the records he had taken. He was barred from entry into the Medical Records department and the specified areas by guards hired to safeguard those remaining medical record documents.

All this medical record tampering and sequestering occurred during the early 1980s, long before HIPPA (Health Insurance Portability and Accountability Act of 1996), the legislation that protected privacy and prevented healthcare fraud was conceived and implemented. Even now, more than thirty years later, it's astonishing to imagine how much abuse and misuse of patient information actually occurred before the advent of electronic medical record technology.

All of us assigned to the litigations were overwhelmed in those early months by the sheer volume of the actual and potential legal actions. Eventually, an additional registered nurse was assigned to assist us in evaluating the increasing numbers of medical records that needed to be reviewed.

In addition to the current litigations, attorneys would contact our department asking for information about many other incidents that would—or would not—evolve into actual legal actions against the medical center. Because these requests didn't specify an actual complaint, just the name and birthdate of the patient, we became medical record detectives, poring over multiple records with minimal clues as to what those attorneys actually wanted.

Our department had already contracted with another registered nurse from Stockton to assist us with transplant cases and other potential cases generated by patients and their families in the areas south of Sacramento. A retired RN in her sixties, Joyce Hampton and I became friends while in Risk Management. We soon realized we could work together effectively and evaluate other medical-legal issues for attorneys not associated in any way with the Medical Center, and we decided to start a consulting firm of our own.

"We can't contact any of the firms with attorneys assigned to cases here at the Medical Center," I told her, "but we can check attorney listings in the phone book and the California Bar Association registry to check out possibilities."

"Why not attorneys here at the Medical Center?"

"There are far too many litigations going on right now in most of the major services, and we have to avoid the possibility of conflict of interest with any of them."

We had no clear idea of how to do it, but in my off-duty hours and on weekends in the last months of 1983 and early 1984, we met with potential attorneys to present our services and go forward as medi-cal-legal consultants. Based on the iconic movie about first-year law students, I suggested Paper Chasers as the name for our firm, and we were off and running.

When Demi Tully, the Acting Risk Manager overseeing my Legal Liaison activities questioned my ethics in starting a consulting ser-vice with the potential for conflicts of interest with the medical center cases, I assured her there would be none. "We already discussed that before we started," I said when she called me into her office to ask me about it.

"Great name, by the way. I wish I'd thought of it."

"Chasing paper is what Joyce and I do here in Risk Management and with our own consulting services. The attorneys we've contacted are not associated with the university or the medical center, and we won't accept any cases that are."

"But Hospital Administration is still concerned. Just be careful and watch your back."

"Our ethics here aren't in question," I said as I got up to leave. "I wonder how ethical it was to have been hired as Transplant Coordinator for a program facing imminent closure, not to have been warned that it would happen, and not to have been thanked—or paid—for taking calls about patient issues here or arranging organ donations at centers in San Francisco for almost two years. You might want to run that by Hospital Administration the next time a question of my ethics comes up."

"You know, I wasn't so sure about taking you on to analyze those transplant cases for our attorneys, but you've been doing a great job here in Risk Management," she said. "I agree you should have been paid for being on-call for all those months, and at least they could have thanked you. These people are not your friends. You and Joyce have a great thing going, but just keep doing everything in Paper Chasers strictly by the book."

It was high time someone saw another side of the Transplant

Program fiasco and realized that I was the last person to be questioned about my medical-legal consulting.

Looking back, it's impossible to believe Joyce and I succeeded in selling the idea that we could assist other attorneys in evaluating and assessing their actual and potential cases for litigation. At first, we did cold calls and unscheduled visits with attorneys who we knew had no association with our UCDMC cases. Joyce also contacted a firm of attorneys in Stockton that liked what we proposed to do and would provide as many cases as we could handle.

We were the precursors of the JD RNs who currently perform the case evaluations that attorneys routinely require involving cases with an emphasis on medical issues. Joyce completed the evaluations that dealt primarily with medical-surgical nursing cases. I also evaluated them but specialized in those dealing with Critical Care and Emergency Care since I had spent the majority of my twenty-plus years in nursing in those specialties.

Joyce was a wonderful colleague, and I enjoyed working with her. The only issue that came between us was the fees we charged. The standard at that time was $100 to $150 per hour for the case evaluations as well as the depositions in which we participated. She declined to testify in court as an expert witness or do depositions, but I did so quite often and enjoyed both.

"I'm fine with the fees they pay me," Joyce told me the day I went over the proposed fee schedule with her. "You have the advanced degrees. I have a three-year diploma in nursing. We'll just do separate billings if that's all right with you."

Despite the differences in opinion about our fees—she never did accept more than $25 per hour for her case evaluations—we worked well together and had permanent sources of assignments with the Stockton firm which specialized primarily in defense of most medical-legal litigations, none of which involved any of the cases originating at the University of California, Davis, Medical Center.

And so it went with my Legal Liaison to Risk Management

assignment at the university and the increasing numbers of cases with Paper Chasers until 1985, when I learned once again how very painful change would be. I had designed the evaluation tool, successfully screened hundreds of possible and actual transplant litigations, and had provided valuable information for our Risk Management Department on many medical-legal issues in other areas specialties for the past two years, but my days at the Medical Center were numbered.

Chapter Eleven

RE-INVENTING ME

IN 1985, DEMI Tully, Acting Director of Risk Management, was passed over for promotion to Risk Manager and decided to move on to graduate school in St. Louis. She had been caustic and contentious with Administration, so no one there was sorry to see her go, but she had been an unexpected ally to me. In her place was a young woman in her twenties with neither Risk Management nor any other type of legal experience, and I was certain she would say or do whatever upper-level management at the University Medical Center dictated.

My resolve to continue Paper Chasers despite the disapproval of that same upper-level management became increasingly difficult. I had focused on the cases that had no link to the university, but one Friday in March, after another cease and desist order regarding my continued consulting and the sudden reassignment of my office space to a colleague who'd wanted it since our move to the building the year before, I finally decided, *That's it! I'm done!*

I went into the office that Sunday, cleared my desk of all personal belongings, left the building for the last time, and never looked back. I still had Paper Chasers and all my nursing skills. I'd survived far worse setbacks than this one, and I would damn well survive the University of California, Davis, Medical Center.

From the transplant program fiasco through assignment to

Hemodialysis and almost two years of unpaid on-call status, from reassignment to Risk Management and constant pressure from Administration to abandon Paper Chasers, I'd finally hit my limit. I was forty-four, I had twenty-three years of professional nursing behind me and was ready to reinvent myself all over again. I had done it in the 1960s, again in the 1970s, and, halfway into the 1980s, I was about to do it again!

If I had changed, so had the delivery of contemporary health care. Intensive Care Units were now standard in all the facilities in my central California city, and the specialty of Emergency Medicine had taken giant leaps forward. I'd been certified and recertified in basic and advanced life support and had stayed current with the technological advances in nursing. Once again, my hands-on care for patients kept me committed to nursing, and the changes in medical supplies and complex equipment remained a constant challenge.

By now, John and I had been married for five years and had finally managed to accomplish the uneasy blending together of our two families. He had never liked my stubborn commitment to my transplant patients, and his only comment about my problems in Risk Management and finally leaving the Medical Center had been a cryptic, "You brought it on yourself." He was no longer supportive and only concerned that, without my full-time position, I might not be able to contribute as well to the family finances. This marriage was worth saving, and I was committed to it, but it was just one more worry added to all the others about where my life was heading.

After leaving the Medical Center, I continued my medical-legal consulting and per diem nursing, precursors of travel nursing companies that proliferated in the 1990s and continue into the present. Our children were growing up. Five of the six were out of the house and on their own, with the youngest still in high school. My older daughter Laura, the mother of my two-year-old granddaughter, was struggling to make a life for the two of them when her own marriage ended.

Ready for another challenge, in the summer of 1985 I answered an

advertisement in one of my nursing journals for a position as a traveling educator, specializing in medical-legal issues and documentation,
a natural with my recent background in risk management and my own
medical-legal consulting experience. The company was based out of
state, and all communications were conducted by telephone or snail
mail, since the internet, as we know it, was not yet available. I met with
the education company director during my in-person interview and
accepted the proposal to teach classes in medical-legal consulting for
one week each month in cities up and down the Eastern Seaboard. By
that September, I was set for the latest adventure.

At first, it was just that, and I enjoyed the challenge, going out and
teaching five classes a week in five different cities, but I soon learned
how grueling that schedule would be. From September through
December 1985, I flew into the first target city on Sunday evening, set
up and taught the class on Monday, then left that evening for the next
city on the schedule, and the next, and the next.

It was exhausting work teaching the class, leaving the hotel for
the airport each evening to catch flights to the next city, and somehow
surviving on next to no sleep. With every trip, I prayed that none of
those flights would leave me stranded or, worse, that I would go down
in flames before I could make it safely home. After the final class, in
Buffalo, New York, in the dead of winter, I knew I'd had enough. It
had been worth the effort to try it, but that job had been a far from
comfortable fit, and it was time to reinvent myself again.

John enjoyed traveling but not all the irritations inherent in actually doing it. When I came home after each trip and told him how
irritating and exhausting it had been, he would just sigh, look at me
as if I were magnifying every problem and ask, "How bad could it be?
You must be exaggerating everything that happened!"

"Then come along with me on the December trip and find out.
Seeing is believing, even if you've already made up your mind."

Certain that I magnified all the problems, he agreed. Seeing how
hard I worked to make the classes a success should have opened his

eyes to how much actual work was involved. Getting to and from all the airports to the hotels, teaching the classes all day for seven hours, then heading to the airport for the next day's class in a different city should have convinced him I had not exaggerated the exhaustion. But he made it anything but easy for me.

By the time I finished the class in Boston and was ready to head to the airport for Buffalo and class the next day, I was ready to leave him there. Nothing that day had pleased him. He hadn't liked waiting all day for me to finish the class and hated having to rush to the airport in time to catch the next flight, for the third time that week.

"Then why did you want to come with me in the first place?" I asked him, at the end of my patience when we arrived in Buffalo in the middle of a snowstorm. "I told you these trips are anything but easy, and I'm not doing this for fun. But if it were your job and I'd come along to help, I'd do it and not spend every single second complaining about it!"

The only thing that made him happy on that trip was the cancellation of the class due to the storm, so we were free the next day to visit Niagara Falls. It was simply beautiful there, and I enjoyed that visit despite the cold and snow, but that trip to the East Coast was my last for that company. I said nothing more to John about the strain of that last trip, but I thought long and hard for the next few years about making any more long-distance trips with him as my constantly complaining companion.

Chapter Twelve

ROAD WARRIOR

I WAS NOW a road warrior, working twelve-hour shifts for nursing registries staffing the Intensive Care and Emergency Departments in healthcare facilities in our central California counties. Always comfortable with basic nursing skills, I recertified in basic and advanced cardiac life support and updated my skills in the ever changing technologies required in modern nursing practice.

Those assignments took me to most of the hospitals in our capital city as well as to the north and as far south as Solano County. Registry nursing generally paid better than staff nursing in those area hospitals, and we didn't need to get involved in any way in hospital politics in any of the facilities in which we were assigned.

That was a plus for me. I'd had enough of political intrigue at the Medical Center in Sacramento and the small community medical center in Roseville. Staff resentments often led to our assignment to the most difficult and demanding patients, and we had no choice but to accept them. Those patients were the ones most likely to require constant personal attention, frequent cardiopulmonary resuscitation when they stopped breathing, the most pumps and monitoring equipment, or the ones with massive infections requiring total shift care by staff wearing gowns, masks, gloves, and all the personal protective equipment that made caring for them so arduous.

Because the registries were utilized to supplement downturns in staffing, we were often called off at the last minute when regular staff became available, and we couldn't count on those hours we had planned to work. I hated those last-minute call-offs, which was why I began considering more permanent positions as they became available.

At the same time, I accepted more consultant cases for Paper Chasers and branched out into doing depositions and testifying at trials in medical malpractice cases. By now, my twenty-fourth year in nursing, I'd survived some incredible challenges and felt so at ease in the courtroom that I began—God help me—to consider applying to law school.

But that went to the back burner for all of 1986 and into 1987 in order to devote myself to family and my now four-year-old grand-daughter, Wendi. I fell for that feisty little baby the moment she was born, and my daughter generously shared her with me as much as possible while supporting both of them as a single parent.

In May 1987, when I received the invitation to attend the twenty-fifth anniversary reunion of the Bellevue Class of 1962 in New York City, I happily accepted. Reluctantly, John came with me. He wasn't interested in the reunion but welcomed the opportunity to see his family. I, on the other hand, had been so preoccupied with my unconventional career that I hadn't attended any of the prior reunions and was curious to see what my former classmates had been up to during those years. A lifetime had passed since graduation, and there was little remaining of that twenty-one-year-old who'd been so sure of her life's direction when she left New York at the end of 1962.

We took time after the reunion to visit John's family in Staten Island and make the trip to Westchester County to show him where I'd lived from the mid-1940s until the mid-1950s. We'd both been born on the East Coast and had lived there through our teens but had never met until that fateful day in California in 1979. In the seventh year of our marriage, we were surviving but were no longer close. John had put everyone in his family first during those years, including his children, brother, sisters, his mother, and even the family priest. His total focus on all of them often excluded me.

"Why did you want to marry me?" I asked him one day when plans for a family party once again didn't include me. "You spend all your time worrying about them and doing everything they ask you to do. They exclude me every way they can, and you go right along with it."

"I do think about you," he insisted. "You don't know what you're talking about." But he kept right on doing it, and I started to focus on my own self-preservation when he stubbornly refused to admit that anything was wrong. In California after the reunion, I spent the winter, spring, and summer working per diem in various health care facilities in the greater Sacramento area and part-time in the small community hospital in Davis. I also saw little Wendi as often as possible.

In the fall of 1987, my daughter Laura entered the academy at the California Department of Corrections in Galt. "Do you think you and John can take Wendi full-time for four months?" she asked when she explained she'd been accepted for correctional officer training. Leroy hadn't found a job and needed to get his act together. Her former husband did love Wendi but couldn't handle the responsibility of being a parent. My husband surprised me by agreeing to care for Wendi while Laura completed the program. His mother, sisters, brother, son John, daughters Lori and Kristen, and assorted nieces and nephews had continued to exclude me and show no interest in Wendi. That was fine with me. I'd given up on all of them four years earlier on the day in 1983 that we attended the christening party for John's youngest nephew, Devon.

Wendi was almost six months old. I'd been babysitting that weekend for Laura and Leroy, off for a weekend together. Wendi was a beautiful baby and good with all the strangers around her, although none of them came near her or asked to hold her. She'd been awake for hours and needed to sleep.

No one I asked, not even John's other sister, mother, and the mother of baby Devon, would help me to find a safe place for her to sleep.

John, as always oblivious, didn't offer to help. It was a moment I would never forget.

Four years later, I loved having that opportunity to spend time with Wendi and was grateful that, this time, John came through. I knew that when Laura started their new life in another part of the state, I would probably see very little of them.

"I'm losing the last links with my own family," I said, tears running down my face as I hugged them both good-bye on the day they left Sacramento. "Tracy doesn't stay in touch, and I never hear from Michael. I'll miss you both so much!"

Laura was assigned to the facility in Avenal after her graduation from the Academy. She and Wendi settled in Coalinga, a small rural city located in the center of the San Andreas Fault, and I worried about earthquakes there as well as their overall safety. By the end of 1987, I had become accustomed to the hole in my life after they left, visited them as often as possible, and continued per diem and part-time nursing assignments. Those days and nights concentrating on my patients kept my mind occupied. John had gone right back to his obsession with his family. All I had now was nursing, and that commitment would save me.

Change had become a constant, and I took on new challenges in a profession that was nothing like it had been at Bellevue twenty-five years before. I still loved patient care in all its permutations and wondered where I would be and what I would be doing when I turned sixty.

Chapter Thirteen

YOU WANT TO
DO *WHAT?*

BY EARLY 1988, I was commuting back and forth among three of the sister hospitals in Sacramento and Davis, keeping busy with Paper Chasers, and beginning again to consider law school. Despite my acceptable GPAs in undergraduate and graduate degree programs at California State University, I realized there was slim to none chance I'd be qualified to enter any of the major California law schools. The LSAT, Law School Aptitude Test, had been a real challenge. I passed it but did only fairly well the first time, and only slightly better the second. An indicator of how I would do in law school if I decided to apply, those LSAT results proved to be a hundred percent correct.

As it turned out, the LSAT exams were nothing compared to the problems that dogged my professional life. Florence Nightingale once wrote, "I attribute my success to this—I never gave or took any excuse." I'd always tried to do as she had done, and, in 1988, for the first time in twenty-six years in nursing, I made a major medication error for which there had been no excuse and for which there could have been devastating consequences.

The past several months, I'd been working in the Emergency Department of one of the larger hospitals in the greater Sacramento area. The nursing staff there had supported the medical director who had made my life miserable whenever we worked together, and I completed each shift waiting for the worst to happen.

One night, when the shift had actually gone well and that particular physician was not on duty, we admitted a patient with chest
pain who was being evaluated for a possible cardiac event. The licensed
vocational nurse who had been assigned to care for him wasn't au-
thorized to provide intravenous potassium, and I was ordered to do
so. Unfamiliar with how it was provided in that facility, and too intimidated by the hostile staff to ask, I gave the correct dose by the
correct route but too quickly, which resulted in a ventricular arrhythmia. The error was corrected immediately, the patient survived, and I
learned a valuable lesson: hostile colleagues or not, my obligation was
to ALWAYS ask for help and not proceed until certain that what I was
doing was absolutely correct. Our patients counted on the professional
staff to keep them safe, and I had let that patient down. I felt terrible,
made no excuses for what I'd done, accepted the three-shift suspen-
sion, and never made the same error again.

When I returned to work in the Emergency Department where
I'd made that error, I remained hyperaware of all potential problems
and was determined to provide the safest care possible, despite the
continued hostility of the medical director and the nursing staff loyal
to him. But several months later, those problems all came to a head,
and a vulnerable patient was placed in jeopardy because of them.

She had given birth several days before and had come in to be examined because she had developed a fever and severe abdominal pain.
I placed her in the Gynecological Exam room, took her initial vital
signs, and performed the basic nursing exam. Her abdomen was taut
and tender to the touch, her temperature was 101 degrees, and blood
pressure, which I'd taken twice on both arms, an alarming 80/60. The
two red flags had been her recent delivery and her abnormal vital signs.
An elevated temperature and alarmingly low blood pressure indicated
a postpartum infection, and she required immediate attention.

The physician on duty that night was the ER physician who'd been
so derisive whenever we worked together. It had been a quiet shift, and

he'd gone to his sleep room several hours earlier with orders not to be disturbed. This patient needed his attention now, so I went ahead and called him. The first time, he ignored the call. The second time, he answered, but before I could say anything, he said, voice icy with disdain, "I told you not to call me, damn it!" and hung up.

The third time, I jumped in before he could say anything. "I have a four-days postpartum patient with abdominal pain, elevated temp, and her blood pressure is 80/60 and falling." He hung up again, refusing to come down to the ED to see her.

None of the staff working that night would buck him, including the Charge Nurse when I told her my concerns. "So why are you telling me? Call him again!" The role of the Charge Nurse is to ensure that care to patients is provided safely and as quickly as possible. This nurse, a personal friend of the physician, didn't check the patient and, like the rest of the staff who supported her and the physician, wouldn't make that call.

Very worried now as I took another set of vital signs and assessed the young woman again, I called the obstetrician who had delivered her baby, reported my assessments, and requested orders for initial lab work, an IV line and fluids, and a stat CT scan.

"Of course, but hasn't the Emergency physician already ordered them?"

In that facility and most others in our area at that time, the ED physician was obligated to see the patient, call the attending physician with suspected diagnosis, his or her recommendations, and request the required labs and diagnostics, medications, and fluids as needed. This woman had had to wait far too long for the on-duty ED physician to examine her, had presented as septic, and had started looking increasingly desperately ill.

"No, he hasn't. That's why I'm calling you." I had already charted the running vital signs and assessments, the calls to the on-duty ED physician, and my report to the Charge Nurse. I drew the blood that the obstetrician ordered, sent it to the Lab, and started two IV lines for more access to fluids and antibiotics, and ordered the CT scan. Once that was done, I called the Administrative Nursing Supervisor to alert her to the likely need for an Intensive Care bed.

"What's going on?" she asked when she arrived in the ED just before the obstetrician.

Wordlessly, I handed her the patient's chart with all the timed notations, and she stormed out to question the Charge Nurse.

When the obstetrician arrived, he confirmed the patient's diagnosis as sepsis and immediately admitted her to Intensive Care. "Why hasn't the physician on duty called me about this patient?" he asked.

I showed him the patient's chart where I had documented the calls made, the refusals to come to the ED to examine the patient, as well as the alarming vital signs, and he took over from there. Apparently, there'd been other complaints about this Emergency Department physician. His inexplicable neglect of this patient had been too serious to ignore, and the Medical Chief of Staff took immediate action.

Dr. G. lost his positions in both Emergency Departments, the Charge Nurse on duty and the staff who had supported her in her refusal to call the ED physician were all reprimanded, and I decided to transfer to another facility. The physician's animosity toward me and the continued hostility of the staff who had supported him and also failed this patient made staying there impossible. Bullying had been integral to my professional life since that long-ago life as a nurse's aide, but this time it had gone too far. That patient needed all of us to fight for her, and the rest of the staff and their Medical Director hadn't done it.

I'd been so worried about that young woman with postpartum sepsis because, just three months earlier, I'd been a member of a team in another Emergency Department. We thought we'd done our best for a young girl who had been admitted with intractable abdominal pain. Initial lab work and exams had all been negative, and she had been discharged home once we had alleviated her pain. One day later, all of us were devastated to learn that she'd died of overwhelming sepsis. We realized, too late, that we had sent her home too soon. All of us experienced in health care delivery, we hadn't recognized the signs of impending sepsis.

That death had been a hard lesson. Today, more than thirty years later, current assessments and technologies, diagnosis and treatment of potential and actual sepsis save many more lives. Still involved in hands-on patient care and a lot more vocal in advocating for my own patients, I remembered that teenage girl who died, that terrified young mother who did not, and, as I neared retirement, I was happy to be working in a medical facility that was in the forefront of diagnosing and treating a medical condition with such potentially devastating consequences.

Chapter Fourteen

WHAT DOESN'T
KILL YOU . . .

IF ANYONE TOLD me that by the end of 1989 I would be juggling nursing positions in two different Sacramento area Emergency Departments, attending monthly Army Reserves meetings, and finishing my first semester in law school, I wouldn't have believed it.

For years I'd felt guilty about that early discharge from the Army Nurse Corps only six months after induction at Fort Sam Houston, Texas. I'd wanted to remain in the Army after the birth of my infant daughter Laura, but the rules about service women remaining on duty with children didn't change until after the mid-1960s.

When a recruiter contacted me in early 1989 about re-joining the Army Nurse Corps, I jumped at the opportunity to devote one weekend a month to the Reserve Unit stationed near my home in Sacramento. I'd been working in the ED in Davis, the rural university city west of Sacramento. One weekend meeting a month shouldn't have been a problem, but the charge nurse, resentful of the Army commitment that she had been told to honor, set about making unexpected changes to my schedule.

With that in mind, I applied for a part-time position in the Emergency Department of the much more challenging sister hospital in Sacramento, with plans to leave the other facility by January 1. I was still working night shifts in both facilities when Kate, a nursing colleague who'd also been considering law school, talked me into applying when she did and starting law school during the summer session. "How hard can it be?" she asked me. "We can give it a try, commit to just two classes, and if we survive with halfway decent grades, we can decide in the fall if we want to continue."

We soon learned just how hard that would be, but, somehow, we survived the two classes we'd chosen that summer and, for better or worse, jumped right into full-time night classes at Lincoln, one of the three law schools in Sacramento.

We didn't apply to the University of Pacific-McGeorge School of Law, the best school in our part of California, because neither of us had shone at either of the two LSATs we'd attempted. I couldn't have afforded the small fortune to earn my law degree there, even if I'd been accepted. Also, McGeorge students weren't permitted to work while attending law school. I needed to pay my own tuition, and I wasn't about to give up my nursing career, so Lincoln became the next best choice.

That September my personal and professional worlds began to collide, and I wondered if it was true that "What doesn't kill you makes you stronger." I was working two night shifts a week at one facility, one shift at the other, spending one weekend each month with the Army Reserves, attending law school from 6 to 9 p.m. three times a week, and completing the Legal Writing class on Saturdays. Too stubborn to give up and determined to meet all those obligations, I staggered on until the end of December that extremely busy 1989, and knew I had to make at least one decision before the beginning of January.

By New Year's Eve, I'd begun to panic about the three final exams looming that first week in January. I almost talked myself into asking for a postponement but knew if I didn't go through with those exams, I'd be finished, in my eyes at least, too mortified to try again.

John and I did go out to celebrate that New Year's Eve at one of the high-end hotels in our capital city. Dressed in an elegant black taffeta dress and the highest heels I could find, I got a lot of leverage out of my law student status with colleagues I hadn't seen since leaving my management position in the small community hospital where John was still employed.

Since then, I'd survived the Transplant fiasco at the Medical Center, the Risk Management drama, the start-up of my own consultation business, and re-induction into the Army Reserves. Law school was just the latest challenge, but even as I celebrated the arrival of a New Year, I knew that talking about law school couldn't dim the cold reality of what it actually was: one of the toughest and most exhausting challenges I had ever undertaken. I did manage to pass all three of those required courses, not with an A or B but the C that many of us had come to accept. They weren't the grades I'd earned at California State University, but I'd survived so far and was ready to face whatever came next.

Author Scott Turow got it right when he wrote *One L* about his first year at Harvard Law School. When I read the book, years after my own One L at Lincoln, I had to admit that he nailed the essence of what it was like to be a law student. He had done it after he completed a baccalaureate degree at Stanford in his twenties and was unemployed when he started law school at Harvard. I'd finished my nursing education at twenty-one, received my undergraduate and graduate degrees in my thirties, began law school at forty-eight, and was now working full-time nights in nursing. His challenges had been nowhere near as daunting as mine.

Most of my fellow classmates at Lincoln also worked, and we all survived somehow on determination, too little sleep, and sheer willpower. What saved me was nursing, the one constant in my life where I continued to thrive, and the change from the small rural Emergency Department to the more intense inner-city one turned out to be a wise decision. I certified as one of the MICNs (Mobile Intensive Care Nurses), handling Fire Department and private ambulance service calls in the evolving paramedical specialty, directing patients to both our facility and our sister hospital across town north of the city.

I worked four ten-hour shifts per week, from 10 p.m. until 8 a.m. Law school classes were held three nights a week from 6 to 9 p.m., and almost always I'd report to work after an especially trying session at Lincoln. My colleagues got used to seeing me studying my huge legal textbooks on the rare occasions we had downtime, and, slowly but surely, I began to think maybe I would survive.

At the end of that first fall semester at Lincoln, I realized I couldn't do justice to my Reserves obligation on the required weekends with all the other obligations that wore me down, so I requested a change in status to the Ready Reserves. It wasn't an easy decision, but with tensions in the Middle East and the threat of war with Iraq, I knew I'd probably stay stateside to relieve activated reservists and still be able to continue law school as well as nursing assignments in Emergency Care.

Chapter Fifteen

... MAKES YOU STRONGER

THE PACE IN that busy Emergency Department ran from stable to frantic. Not the designated trauma center for our capital city, we did receive a fairly considerable number of actual trauma victims who required stabilization before going on for more definitive care at University of California, Davis, Medical Center. One of them arrived on a frantic night when we'd already had two other gravely ill patients requiring immediate cardiopulmonary resuscitation. This patient arrived with a bullet wound in his right atrium. Fortunately for him, our entire staff had been Trauma Nurse certified the week before. We, and the young surgeon who plugged the wound with his finger until we could get the man to surgery, were able to do our best to save him.

Due to the constant need to provide rapid care and disposition for our patients, I became even more experienced at all aspects of ED care, from Triage through both the cardiac and stroke interventions that had become standard. After my law school classes ended at 9 p.m., I'd arrive at the ED, change into scrubs, and be ready to accept my assignments by 10 p.m.

We were almost always extremely busy, with two Resuscitation Rooms off the main lobby, three ED beds across the front of the large open room, three across the back, four private rooms with doors down the right side, and four more in the back of the ED, one of which was reserved for gynecological exams. The pace was constant, with no set time for breaks, but whenever there was a lull, I'd be reading case law in one of the many courses currently assigned at Lincoln. If possible, usually no earlier than 4 a.m., I'd head back to the Radiology Waiting Room, sit back on one of the couches and close my eyes for half an hour. It was usually enough to recharge my brain and body for the next few hours until I was off duty at 8 a.m. That only happened if no new patients came in between 7 and 8 a.m. or I wasn't needed to relieve the day shift nurses who took breaks as soon as they came into the Emergency Department.

Then 1990 became 1991, and, just to make my life even more miserable, I had to undergo a second breast needle biopsy. I'd had the first in the fall of my first year at Lincoln, had been distraught at the possibility of breast cancer, and was as mad as hell that it had happened to me again.

The second biopsy, like the first, was negative. The diagnosis of fibrotic breast tissue was a huge relief, but I still worried. I couldn't waste a minute. When given the all-clear by my physician, I returned to my ED duties and law school classes with a vengeance.

"Look to the right and to the left of you," one of our instructors told us when we started law school. "Only one of the three of you will still be there at the end of your second year." For my friend Kate and me, Real Property, a totally incomprehensible area of law, became our personal Waterloo. In our trio of stressed students, only Evelyn, a sixty-year-old grandmother with a doctorate in music education and who taught at California State University, was still standing.

Kate and I hadn't failed Real Property, but because we'd just barely survived it, our grade point averages were too low to permit us to continue at Lincoln. We could take Real Property again and try to raise our grades or, with the other nineteen men and women in our class still struggling to survive, move on to the friendlier, more nurturing law school founded a few years earlier by a judge, Lorenzo Patiño, shortly before he died of leukemia.

Now co-owned by his widow and a well-known area bail bonds-man, the University of Northern California Lorenzo Patiño School of Law, which I fondly called the Fly-by-Night School of Law, made life a little easier as we started our third year. Judge Patiño had written, "This is a law school where people can study law, prepare for the Bar and a future in law, yet do so affordably, a no-frills law school." He'd had the right idea. UNC became a haven for all of us who transferred there in the fall of 1991.

Law school was expensive, even at UNC. Kate was married to a physician, had no worries about how to pay for her legal education, and thought the study of law would be "interesting." I had no illusions about law or attorneys since I'd been working with them for five years by the time I started at Lincoln. I was able to pay my own tuition and had never yet turned down a challenge. I knew those four years of law school at night would be tough, but when anyone dared tell me, "Young lady, you'll never be able to survive it," I'd just smile, thank him or her, and become even more determined to succeed.

My life was now a little less stressful, except for the increasing tension at home. I was always exhausted, often overwhelmed by the need to excel in school and work and still maintain a household. There was no support from my husband, who continued putting his family first and me last. I was succeeding in a profession that he and his family resented and didn't understand. I had respect and admiration from colleagues and friends, but none at home, and by the beginning of 1991, I knew it would never change. I would finish law school. I would not give up on this complicated second marriage. I would survive, but I knew it wouldn't be easy.

Chapter Sixteen

THOUSAND-MILE JOURNEY

OUR NEW LAW school was located in an office building on J Street, near Macy's and its adjacent mall, and we attended classes there for the first of our last two years at UNC. We would have continued in that location, but the owner of the building decided to sell it, and the law school owners were obliged to search for another site.

In January of that same year, Kate alerted me to an advertisement she'd seen in the *Sacramento Bee*. "It looks perfect for you," she said. "The California District Attorneys Association is looking for someone with a background in writing to assist with editing legal publications here in Sacramento. It's a legal internship with no pay, but it's just right for you."

"But what about you? Why don't you apply?"

"Because you're the one who can write. You know you can do it, so just go for it!"

The fact that I was a law student was a plus. Writing had saved me in law school. For the past three years, every one of our quizzes and exams had been completed in our Blue Books, just as they had been at California State University. As certain as I was that I would never enjoy law as well as I had enjoyed writers and poets, I knew I could write about it and edit what attorneys in northern California wrote about it.

I took Kate's advice, applied for the position, and, before I knew it,

I was a legal intern editing articles written by district attorneys on all aspects of Criminal Law. This unpaid internship earned me additional law school credits at UNC, fourteen more than the eighty required for the Juris Doctor degree, and my name as associate editor in a book on criminal trial tactics.

That final year at UNC, I became secretary for our class, which included coordinating our graduation ceremony and celebration. I don't know why I decided to take it on, but I was in this latest obsession until the end, and I wanted to make the most of those years, even if I never pursued a career in law.

As always, nursing provided a balance. I knew what I had to do to keep patients alive and comfortable, but it was an intense double life of dedicated professional nurse and struggling law student. Strangely, although I was exhausted, I never felt more alive. At twenty and twenty-one, finishing my final year at Bellevue and editing our once-a-month *Starch and Stripes,* I had felt similar stress, but this life of constant challenges was both more daunting and more rewarding than I had ever anticipated.

Law school and law students moved again for the final year of our four-year program to an older building on J Street, a mile south of the present one. Encompassing the second floor of the building housing restaurants and small businesses beneath it, our classes could be reached only by an incredibly steep set of twenty wooden stairs, an inevitable accident waiting to happen.

"You've got to be kidding!" I told Kate the first time I saw those stairs. "If anyone is going to fall, it'll probably be me!" Fortunately, that never happened. I had slipped on the stairs in our previous building, bruising my sternum on the metal railing, but had not bounced all the way down to the bottom. This time I would be more vigilant.

The second floor housed several small classrooms, meeting rooms, and an amphitheater with tiered seating where we attended most of our classes, held meetings, and spent three evenings a week for the final nine months of our program. I reported in at least once a week for my editing assignments at the offices of the District Attorneys Association in Sacramento and continued my four ten-hour shifts each week at the general hospital adjacent to the Interstate 80 freeway that ran north and south of Sacramento.

That last year was my busiest. No novice at juggling an increasingly complex life, I looked forward to completing the program and facing whatever came next. I wasn't sure what I would do with the law degree, but I was determined to complete it, and as the class member designated to orchestrate our graduation ceremony and celebration, I got caught up in that event as well.

We all wanted a graduation program in which we had a voice, and my job had been to locate a venue that would both make our graduation memorable and that we could afford with the funds the owners could provide. In the end, they agreed to one that would honor all of us. The class officers approved the plan, the law school owners agreed to pay the matching funds, and we were set for the event at Capital Plaza Halls on May 23, 1993.

Because of my writing background, my classmates asked me to write the message to be included in our commencement program. Committed to providing a personal memory for all of us who had worked so hard, I finally wrote: "A journey of a thousand miles begins with a single step. For us graduating here today, our journey began with a series of steps, not one, and for us, those thousand miles seemed more like ten thousand, most of them uphill."

I went on to write about how going on had often been the toughest decisions we had to make and borrowed the final words from the speech by former President Calvin Coolidge: "Nothing in the world will take the place of persistence," he'd said. "Talent will not—nothing is more common than unsuccessful men with talent. Genius will not—unrewarded genius is almost a proverb. Education will not—the world is full of educated derelicts. Persistence and determination alone are omnipotent."

Those words applied to all of us who graduated that Sunday in

May. The ceremony was a success and so was the reception that followed, each of us joined by families, friends, and former classmates at Lincoln, who had celebrated their own graduation the week before. We were role models for those law students coming after us and for family and friends who had supported and encouraged us throughout those incredible four years. For us, in the lives we led and the goals we pursued in addition to law school, it had been the most challenging journey we had so far undertaken.

Chapter Seventeen

MOVING ON

IN CALIFORNIA IN the 1990s, only fifty percent of law school graduates who took the Bar Exam passed the first time. I was not one of them. For me, not passing felt like the worst kind of failure. Awarded a Bar Exam Review Course for my work as class secretary, I knew I probably would have been better off studying that for the next five months and waiting until January to take the exam itself. Exhausted after the double life of working hard and studying even harder those four long years, anxious to clear that final hurdle, I foolishly went ahead and took the exam in July.

Sitting for that exam and knowing that half of us there would not make the cut was an ordeal. For me, it was more a matter of pride. I already had a satisfying career, with a position waiting for me in Emergency nursing. With none waiting for me in the legal profession after four years as a law student, I wasn't at all certain I wanted one, but that dreaded bar exam still constituted the final hurdle. Ironically, I missed passing it that first time by only ten points. When the results were posted in December, I swallowed my disappointment and went right back to studying for the next one, scheduled in January.

I never did manage to pass it, and, by 1995, I decided that enough was enough. I was almost fifty-four, had found my niche in Emergency nursing, and presumed that some Higher Being had other plans for me. I had no idea what they were or how I'd manage to achieve them, but the legal profession would have to have one less lawyer, and I suspected that pursuing other goals would make me happier.

It had been years since I'd sat down and written something besides those required projects for my undergraduate and graduate programs at California State University, Sacramento. Law school exams were just rewritten exercises in black letter law and didn't count. So, in 1995, I started to think about taking a turn at fiction. Good books by good writers had saved my sanity during those stressful years before and after law school, and now was the time to get going on the mystery novel that would begin the next challenge in a life already rich with them.

Still working full-time night shifts in Emergency, I began filling page after page on lined yellow legal tablets. I'd been thinking about the administrative aspects of nursing, what did or did not work, what aspects of my career had been problematic for me, and what in the world would interest anyone besides those actively involved in health careers. Starting with a working title that would carry my two protagonists from past to present, I took a year to complete the first draft of *Past Forgetting* and a second year to edit and complete the second draft.

I'd always wanted to write novels, and *Past Forgetting* became my fourth attempt at one that was potentially publishable. I hadn't succeeded with *Army Daze,* written at thirty while recuperating from my broken knee. The Master's thesis at California State University, also a novel, earned me the MA in Creative Writing but was nowhere near good enough to send out, and neither was a third forgettable contemporary novel.

Past Forgetting had a chance, but completing it left me tremendously let down. I'd done it, finished what I'd put off for so long, but didn't have the energy to look for an agent or publisher, so I set it aside and continued pursuing my unconventional career in nursing.

By then, it was 1998. The Emergency Department in which I'd been working had undergone quite a few administrative changes.

Sadly, the young ED director who had hired me had died of esophageal cancer the year after I'd completed law school. She'd been only
thirty-one and the mother of a two-year-old daughter. That tragedy
had shaken all of us. What made work harder to take was the appointment of subsequent directors, none of whom had her dedication,
energy, or management skills.

I'd begun to branch out with per diem assignments in other facilities and in other areas of nursing, including on-call in a local Post-
Anesthesia Care unit (PACU). I enjoyed the challenge but not that I'd
be working alone with multiple admissions and no backup when it was
needed. One evening toward the end of my three-month assignment
there, I was notified that I'd be receiving back-to-back patients who
required arterial line monitoring, and when I called my supervisor and
then the ICU staff to assist in setting up the equipment while I recovered my other patients, I was told I was on my own.

This was a faith-based medical facility, but one in which some
managers and staff put the needs of the patients last and their own
needs first. It had happened several years before when, as a travel nurse,
I had worked several shifts in Intensive Care in the same facility and
had asked for assistance with one of my patients when dealing with an
emergency with a second one. "It's your problem, not mine" the supervisor told me then, and now, responding to my call, the Charge Nurse
in ICU ordered me to "Just handle it."

Post-anesthesia patients require careful monitoring, and one staff
member shouldn't be left alone to do it. That night I decided that
PACU, at least in that facility, was not for me. I set up the equipment
and recovered the patients without any assistance, completed one more
on-call shift and resigned, not about to work anywhere again where
nursing colleagues didn't help each other for the benefit of the patients
who needed them.

By then, the northern Sacramento community hospital where
I'd worked in the early 1980s had become the most recent addition to one of the three area health care organizations and a new,

state-of-the-art facility that had been built. I continued working in the older Sacramento facility and, at the request of the new facility nursing director, also provided extra night shifts in the ED when needed. Both facilities were under the same financial umbrella, and administrators in both eventually realized that those extra shifts constituted overtime.

I'd volunteered to work those shifts assuming they were straight time but was happy to receive the substantial remuneration. I was also happy to leave that inner-city Sacramento hospital where most of my colleagues didn't seem happy in their chosen profession. What made it worse was that so many of them put their own needs first and resented the patients they were committed to care for. When offered the opportunity to move on to the new facility, I didn't hesitate.

Chapter Eighteen

MOVING ON AGAIN

WHEN I MADE the official change to the newer, larger, and more functional ED in the sister hospital north of the city, I returned to the facility where I completed all the per diem overtime shifts. For the most part, it was an easy transition. Lisa, the nurse manager, knew me from the old days in the community hospital where she'd been a nurse just starting her career in ICU, and I had been her director. The ED physicians and staff seemed happy in their new facility, and most of them welcomed me back.

Only one of them, Dan W., made those night shifts in ED a little difficult. Gone for the past year from the old ED, he came back to the new one assuming he'd always be in charge. We were two of the three assigned to do so, and on one of my assigned nights as charge nurse, after I had already received the change of shift report, he arrived late and attempted to take charge. When the other staff members went off to their assigned areas, I pulled Dan aside.

"We went over this last week in the staff meeting," I reminded him. "You, Tom, and I rotate our charge nurse duties while we certify as Clinical Nurse IIIs. Tom was in charge on Tuesday, you were in charge yesterday, and I'm in charge today, so let's just get to work. Don't make me have to call Lisa to sort this out. We have patients waiting."

Tom S., the other designated charge nurse and Dan's polar opposite, always accepted his charge assignments graciously, enjoyed hands-on nursing whereas Dan did not, and served as a mentor and role model for all new staff. I also enjoyed getting through those often overwhelming shifts as charge nurse and provider of hands-on care. Dan eventually did adhere to the rotating charge nurse schedule that the director provided, but working with him remained stressful. He was not at heart a team player and wanted to spend most of his on-duty with the Emergency physicians. I would have rather worked with anyone else.

I enjoyed the physical plan of the new ED far more than the one in which I'd worked for so many years in Sacramento. A large waiting room was just off the main entrance, with a Triage desk where we all took turns answering the Triage bell. Our mantra was to keep no one waiting, and we spent a great part of each shift triaging those patients who required immediate attention.

Triage opened directly into the main ED work area, surrounded on all sides by patient rooms and cubicles. Down the right hallway were two private rooms, one devoted to gynecological patients. Down the hallway leading directly from the ambulance bay were two resuscitation rooms for our cardiac, stroke, and major trauma patients. In the back hall were two more private exam rooms and, to the right of them, the large open room where we cared for patients awaiting admission or further workups following their initial examination and treatment.

Most of those patients were elderly with multiple comorbidities requiring more than just emergency care. For the time that I was employed there, those holding beds were almost always filled. For those nurses who wanted only the pace and excitement of emergency patient care, those assignments to ED Holding led to unhappiness and resentment. I actually enjoyed the myriad challenges that ED Holding presented. For the most part, we had excellent teamwork. On one particularly stressful night, the Vice-President for Nursing came down to the overcrowded unit to help. It had been many years since she had provided hands-on patient care, but she helped alleviate our stress just by being there.

This was a community medical center in a populous city north of Sacramento, and since it provided direct links to Interstate 80, we saw a significant number of trauma patients. It was also a designated cardiovascular and stroke facility, so we treated a large number of cardiac and neuro patients as well.

One of the most memorable was a feisty little woman in her eighties diagnosed with a dissecting thoracic aortic aneurysm. She had never been in a helicopter but had the ride of her life that night when she was evacuated by air to the University Medical Center Trauma Unit in Sacramento. Unfortunately, the dissection had become too severe, and she didn't survive long enough to undergo surgery. Brave to the end, she'd chosen that helicopter ride as her final adventure in a long and productive life, and we cheered her on as she took off on that epic flight.

We had many more incredible moments in those years between 1998 and 2000, some of which have remained clearly in my memory. One night we had side by side patients with catastrophic injuries while I was precepting a nursing student completing her last semester. In two weeks, she'd be starting her new career in one of the hospitals in the Sacramento area, and this night would be one of her most memorable as a nursing student.

Tom, in charge that night, took the radio call and announced, "Listen up! We're getting two victims of gunshot wounds, both undergoing CPR!" With the rest of the staff assigned to the Trauma Rooms, we prepared to try to save them both. We did save the seventeen-year-old girl, victim of a home invasion, but couldn't save the young man, a family friend who had jumped in front of her when one of the assailants pulled out a gun and begun firing. One bullet went straight into his heart, but he'd been able to deflect the second shot that went into her right chest. She lived, but he died. It was a painful lesson for the new nurse to learn that, despite all our efforts, he had been beyond saving.

In January 2001, I was promoted to ED Clinical Nurse III. I loved my role in that fast-paced Emergency Department but had begun looking for experience in other areas as well. I applied for a position as Administrative Nurse Supervisor, and when one became available on the night shift, I accepted it. Incorporating all my past and present accomplishments in nursing, it would propel me from one set of problems in one patient care setting to a vast set of even more complicated ones that involved the entire medical center. And I was ready.

Chapter Nineteen

FINALLY FINDING MY NICHE

I WAS HIRED part-time to replace a colleague who'd taken a position in another hospital, and I worked as often as they needed me. My goal was to learn all the elements of the position as quickly as possible, including orientation to the areas of the medical center I hadn't yet seen while working in the Emergency Department. Because I'd worked in the old facility, I already knew most of the staff in the present one, and my fellow supervisors and immediate manager, the Director of Nursing Operations, were accepting and supportive. Unfortunately, that didn't apply to everyone.

Healthcare is a little like the military: you're likely to run into some people over and over again and not always in a good way. One of them was Mariah Bell. We'd met almost twenty years before, when I was Critical Care Educator at the University Medical Center in Sacramento. She was in her twenties, working in the Medical Intensive Care Unit; I was in my thirties and just developing the Critical Care Orientation Program. We shared a distant relationship when I worked with her again several years later in Medical Intensive Care, where I provided emergency dialysis sessions for renal failure patients after their transplants failed.

I'd gone on to my role in Risk Management, she'd moved on to one of the other acute care facilities in our capital city, and I didn't run into her again until the 1990s. By then, I'd survived many upheavals in my professional life, completed law school, and was working full-time night shifts in Emergency nursing. Our young ED director had esophageal cancer and couldn't return to her duties in the Emergency Department. Taking her place as Interim Director was "some nurse who doesn't have a clue about Emergency nursing," as several of my colleagues who had worked with her in the past told me. "She looks like Betty Boop and talks like a ditzy teenager," they continued. I was amused when it turned out to be Mariah.

Amusement ended as she took on her new duties. She'd never worked in Emergency nursing, resented all of us who were far better prepared, and denied that she'd gotten the position due to the influence of a physician friend with whom she worked in a small community hospital in the Sierra foothills. She remembered me from the old days at the Medical Center. She hadn't liked me then and liked me even less now because of my expertise in Emergency nursing compared to her own. More than that, she didn't like being reminded that I graduated from law school when she had failed in her first year. She actually told me the first week she was there, "I knew you'd never pass the bar exam."

Already insecure, she focused her frustrations on me and made our few shifts together pure misery as she oriented to the Emergency Department. A year later, not appointed the permanent ED Director because she hadn't convinced the staff and Medical Director that she could do the job, she went back to her prior role in the other facility in the foothills. I didn't run into her again until a few years later, after I'd taken the Emergency nurse position in the medical center in Roseville.

Mariah had been working there as day shift Administrative Supervisor for the past year, and our paths had rarely crossed. Then I accepted the position as the Administrative Supervisor and was required to work with her again. Never a warm or empathetic person, she remembered our prior interactions and made it clear she didn't want me in the Administrative Supervisor role. The year before, during my Clinical RN III assignment in the Roseville ED, she'd balked at the order for an Observation Unit admission for my husband John, who'd had a painful renal lithotripsy procedure late that afternoon.

The intravenous analgesic provided following the procedure had not minimized his pain by the time it came to discharge him home. Usually stoic, and with no history of the type of pain he was now experiencing, there was no way he would recover well at home. As we lived twenty-five miles away, the Post-Anesthesia Care nurses agreed that he required closer monitoring, but still Mariah balked.

"Why can't you watch him at home? It was just a lithotripsy. Surely, you can manage that."

"And, surely, you know that if you don't get the bed in the Observation unit, Dr. Keith will hear about it. He ordered it. You know as well as I do that all patients receiving Dilaudid require closer monitoring."

She did know. The administration of Dilaudid, three times stronger than morphine, had resulted in near fatal or fatal reactions at our facility and others in our area. If John's blood pressure and respiratory status weren't closely monitored after it was administered, he would be at risk as well.

"But he's an outpatient!" she snapped, exasperated that Dr. Keith had ordered the admission and that the Post-Anesthesia Care Unit nurses had called him at my request.

"He was an outpatient. Now, he's not; I know you'll take care of this as soon as you can." She took care of it because she had no reason not to, and she even liked my husband, who had been on staff at that hospital for more than thirty-five years. She'd been wrong to dispute the admission because she didn't like me, and in all the time I'd known her, Mariah had never admitted being wrong about anything.

Now, during orientation to the Administrative Supervisor role when she relieved me in the mornings, she found fault with everything I'd done the night before. One major problem that faced all of us as Nursing Supervisors was the continued lack of sufficient staff due to call-offs, scheduling mistakes, and the plethora of problems that impacted all the patient care areas in our busy medical center.

After Mariah told me I was incompetent one morning when a staff nurse in Telemetry didn't report to work, I'd had enough. "You gave her the day off yesterday," I reminded her. "I heard you talking with her when she called in about a death in her family."

Mistakes happen. I'd made enough during my many years in nursing and forgotten none of them. Mariah decided to blame me for this one, but I wouldn't go to war with her over it. Without another word, I called a per diem RN, asked her to work for her team member, then placed a call to the Director of Nursing Operations to set up an intervention.

Mariah had made numerous mistakes in scheduling while she oriented me and consistently blamed the nursing staff for the errors. Many of them saw her as officious and flighty and said she never supported them when other issues arose with physicians and management. I was a thorn in her side because I did support the staff and went out of my way to keep dissension to a minimum.

Aware of Mariah's problems with staff and her antagonism toward me, the Director of Nursing Operations strongly advised us to learn to get along. The situation finally resolved itself when Mariah was given the position of Risk Manager. She had no experience in that specialty, and her promotion puzzled everyone, but I was very happy to see her leave. The Administrative Supervisor role was still mine, and I could finally enjoy the position I was working so hard to master.

Chapter Twenty

THE QUEENS
OF MEAN

YOU FIND THEM everywhere: nurses who eat their young and often the older colleagues with whom they work. While Mariah might have been critical and obstructive to me in my new role as Administrative Supervisor, there'd been many more just like her during my unconventional career. I called them the Queens of Mean, nurses and support personnel who far surpassed former hotelier Leona Helmsley in their treatment of the people with whom they worked.

I hadn't forgotten the charge nurse in the Neurological Intensive Care Unit at University of California, Davis, Medical Center who slapped me across the face when I'd asked which of her staff would be attending the Critical Care Orientation Course mandated by her Director. She hadn't wanted her staff to participate, had taken her frustrations out on me, and when I encountered her years after leaving the medical center, she acted as if it had never happened.

Because I'd left my prior position in the downtown Sacramento facility to take the one in Roseville in 2001, I also applied for and was accepted as a per diem staff nurse in the Emergency Department Per Diem Pool at another of the major medical facilities in our area. As always, that challenge became more than I'd bargained for, and the Queens of Mean in that department made night shifts pure agony.

I had worked per diem shifts in the Intensive Care Units as a

Registry nurse in that facility but had never experienced the malice some staff exhibited toward their coworkers in the Emergency Department. It was one of the older established ones in which I'd worked and was almost always overrun with patients. There were two major hallways off the primary admitting area, with the one on the left devoted to the more critical patients requiring monitoring and ending at the six-bed unit at the rear. Down the opposite side and bounded by the admitting desk for that hallway were the Gynecological Exam Room and a second six-bed room for holding our non-critical patients. Lined up along that hallway and often ignored by the staff were patients awaiting their examinations or dispositions, often crying or attempting to climb off the uncomfortable and inadequate stretchers, sometimes waiting for hours for attention.

Many of the nursing staff in that department put themselves first and the patients last. That healthcare facility supported the union for professional nurses, and it always seemed ironic that, for them, higher salaries and better benefits didn't guarantee better care for the patients. I worked there on a per diem basis, tried my best to avoid politics and focus on patient care, but that wasn't always possible.

The charge nurse was male, reputed to be the best they ever had, but, like many others who worked there for years, he didn't put the welfare of the patients first. Married to a Radiology technician who consistently complained to him about the nurses, he spent most of his shifts in Radiology with her and not in the Emergency Department.

As a per diem staff member, I was assigned to all the areas in that ED, and often needed to question the care provided to those patients. That health care system triaged the patients quickly, treated them as needed, then sent them home as soon as possible. This wasn't always in their best interests. Physicians and nurses who worked those night shifts weren't happy to be challenged about their rule to "treat and street." As long as I worked there, I was one of the few who did, usually with good cause but not always with the best results.

One elderly man, having problems with his arteriovenous fistula, required admission and closer monitoring. I'd kept him in the six-bed unit in the acute section of the ED as long as possible but hadn't succeeded in convincing his physician to continue monitoring him closely in the ED or have him admitted to one of the Intensive Care Units for observation.

Working in the Dialysis Unit at the University Medical Center years before, I'd learned how serious leaking fistulas could become. Although I was concerned that the fistula would fail, I reluctantly sent the man home when the ED physician and Charge Nurse demanded it. Several hours later, before my shift ended, he was brought back into the Emergency Department in full cardiac arrest after the fistula ruptured and he exsanguinated before his frantic family could save him. I never forgot him or that I'd been the one who sent him home, and I vowed I would never again fail to fight harder for a patient.

Not long after that, I refused to discharge a woman who came in to be checked for continued abdominal pain after exploratory surgery. The physician who examined her had found nothing to explain the pain, provided a stronger analgesic prescription, and then ordered the patient's discharge from the unmonitored side of the Emergency Department.

She just hadn't looked right to me. Her blood pressure had been low on triage and remained low throughout her visit. When I took her discharge vital signs, I was alarmed to see it at 85/50 and her heart rate at 130. Her skin was cool and clammy. When I reported all this to the charge nurse in that area, I was told to discharge her anyway.

"She has discharge orders, so discharge her! We need that room, and we need it now!" An unhappy Licensed Vocational Nurse who frequently assumed control of that side of the ED through sheer intimidation, she walked away and assumed that I would do as told.

Instead, I immediately placed the woman on a stretcher, rolled her over to the monitored side of the ED and obtained an EKG. I suspected sepsis due to her alarming vital signs and how gravely ill she looked as I prepared to discharge her. I was criticized by some other colleagues who also told me to send her home, but the EKG clearly indicated an acute cardiac injury. Post-operative sepsis was also diagnosed, and she was admitted to Intensive Care. If she'd gone home as ordered, she probably wouldn't have survived.

"Why did you decide to get that EKG?" the doctor who had ordered her discharge asked me after the cardiologist consulted with her. "And why didn't you just discharge her in the first place? You know she owes you her life to you."

"The most important thing I learned from the best doctors and nurses at Bellevue was to always trust my instincts."

Another battle fought—and won—involved a middle-aged man who survived polio as a child, overcame considerable disabilities, and rehabilitated himself, only to be transported to the Emergency Department with a tibial-fibular fracture of his stronger leg. Rather than place a temporary splint and keep him overnight, the physician and other ED staff insisted that this man could go home on his own, with no one to help him on that long holiday weekend, and could come back in several days for the permanent cast. With no caseworker or social service staff there to back me up, I finally convinced the ED physician to do the right thing, call the orthopedist, and have the patient admitted until arrangements could be made for home care.

Those dying patients with Do Not Resuscitate orders whom we often evaluated in that ED were seen as problems that many staff didn't want to address. One night after I'd just come on duty, an elderly woman arrived on the non-critical side of the department. Her daughter couldn't face the imminent death and had left her alone in the offside exam room where the EMTs had placed her. There was a brief lull in ED admissions that night, and since I hadn't yet received my assignment, I told the charge nurse I'd stay with her.

"Absolutely not!" he told me. "You're needed for patients we *can* resuscitate."

I ignored him, went over his head, and called the supervisor on duty to override his objections. Patients were always my priority. I was damned if I would let this uncaring, poor excuse for a charge nurse stop me from easing a patient's last moments just because he had the power to do it.

I stayed with her, easing her last moments until she died half an hour later. It hadn't made me popular that night or in the year that I remained in that Emergency Department, but advocating for patients who couldn't fight for themselves had been ingrained in all those years in nursing, and as tough as it had always been to stand my ground, I'd done it. What are we here for if it's not to take care of each other? I knew someday I could be that little old woman, left to die alone. I wouldn't wish that kind of death for anyone.

Chapter Twenty-One

SEPTEMBER 11, 2001

NEITHER I NOR my sisters Carroll and Jeanie made it to North Carolina in time to be with our mother before she died. She was admitted to the hospital in early July 2000 due to respiratory problems that had plagued her most of her adult life. After our father died two years earlier, she refused to leave North Carolina to live with any of us. We would have gladly welcomed her—in California, Illinois, or Connecticut—but she firmly resisted. Independent till the end, stubbornly refusing to be a burden, she went into respiratory failure and died before any of us could reach her bedside.

Of the three of us, my mother's death saddened me the most. Adventurous as she'd been in her early life, she'd cheered me on in my own adventures and accomplishments and told me that someday I would come into my own in more ways than I ever imagined. Unable to tell her how much she inspired me and believed in me has haunted me since her death in 2000, and in her memory, I tried to always take extra time and provide special attention to all of the elderly patients who came into my care.

One of her final wishes was that we scatter her ashes over the ocean near the city in North Carolina near where she and my father retired twenty years before. One year after her death, we all planned to meet in Wilmington to carry out her request. Carroll would fly in from

Connecticut, Jeanie from Illinois, and I from California. When we left our respective homes on that September 9 for our final goodbye, we had no idea that, two days later, our journeys would end in a turning point for us and for everyone in our country.

I arrived after 10 p.m. in Raleigh-Durham on September 9 planning to make what should have been an easy trip down to Wilmington. Exhausted by the long trip, I was not at all prepared for what happened on that isolated road leading away from the airport.

It was just after 10:30 that I heard it, a sudden, solid THUNK as something (I thought) fell out of the sky, slammed into the hood, and totally obscured the windshield. Terrified, I stopped the car and hunkered down in my seat and prayed that would be the end of it. When I finally found the courage to get out of the car, I walked around to the front and saw the latch that secured the hood had loosened and broken open, slamming it back against the windshield.

"I don't have time for this!" I said aloud, with absolutely no one around to hear me. Since I couldn't budge that tightly wedged hood and couldn't see enough to drive, I called the number on the car rental form. No one answered at the rental kiosk at the airport, and no one who passed me on that isolated road stopped to help.

What do I do now? I wondered. This was just the latest in one unending challenge after another. I finally decided to call 911. Someone in Raleigh-Durham could probably figure out what to do.

I dialed what I thought was 911 on the flip phone I used only for emergencies and was amazed when my husband, back home in California, answered. "What have you gotten yourself into this time?" he asked before I could tell him what had happened. It struck my last nerve, his assumption that, once again, I'd done something stupid. In our twenty-one-year marriage, he'd become really good at that, and I'd given up asking for his help when something went wrong. Already at the end of my patience after the long flight and longer delays at the two other airports where he'd arranged my complicated connections, I hung up before he could say anything else. He could have at least asked if I'd been injured.

Determined to find someone to help, I searched through the rental agreement again, found the national help line number for the car agency and dialed. Thankfully, someone did respond, called a local number for me, and sent agents to the airport to rescue me and provide another car.

When that was accomplished, I was back on the road again, still exhausted and thoroughly shaken. It was now after midnight September 10 in North Carolina, and it had begun to rain heavily. In an unfamiliar car on unfamiliar highways, I made the final leg of the journey, convinced I'd be the third member of my family to die in North Carolina. I finally made it safely to the hotel in downtown Wilmington at 4 a.m., fingers crossed that they'd saved my room when I hadn't reconfirmed the reservation.

Due to meet with my sisters at 8 a.m., I finally fell into bed at 5 a.m., still wearing all the clothes I'd traveled in. Less than three hours later, I did what I could with my hair and makeup and met my sisters for breakfast.

"Not exactly beach wear!" my younger sister announced, ready as always to criticize. Some battles were just not worth fighting, and, besides, she was right. I hadn't had the energy to look for something else to wear when I woke up and now looked as awful as I felt. "Long trip," I told them both as I yawned repeatedly and drank cup after cup of coffee, as strong and as hot as I could stand it.

Then, at a little after 9 a.m., the three of us set off for the beach, where for years our mother had collected shells during the time she and our father lived there. We cried as her ashes—all that was left of her—lifted up and flew out over the waves.

Emotionally and physically drained, we went back to the hotel, where Jeanie prepared to fly back to Illinois that afternoon, Carroll prepared for her trip north the next day, and I rested up for my flight back to California, planning to leave several hours after she did. It was now noon.

The next day was September 11. Carroll and I had breakfast that Tuesday morning and were on our way upstairs to get ready for our respective journeys home when she stopped on the stairs and pointed. "Oh, my God! Look at that!" she cried out as we witnessed on the TV screens around us the unbelievable tragedy that had begun to unfold in New York City.

At first, like everyone else, we thought that the first plane had struck the Trade Center by accident. It had happened once before in New York City in the 1940s, when a small plane had struck the Empire State Building. Had the unbelievable happened again? But as we watched in horror when the second plane struck the second tower, we all knew we were witnessing the end of the safe and secure existence we had always taken for granted in our country.

I hadn't been in New York when the Twin Towers were built and had only been back a few times since heading out west in my twenties. But New York had once been my city, and I had myriad memories of my three years there as I'd learned the craft of nursing. All that endless day, from the safety of Wilmington, North Carolina, I prayed for everyone caught up in the death and devastation and for my fellow healthcare providers who would somehow have to deal with the aftermath.

Carroll and I watched television all that long and dreadful day, still safe in Wilmington, but anxious to get to our families All the airports across the country had closed, and all flights were canceled. She wouldn't be able to get back to her family in Connecticut, nor I to mine in California, until the potential threat to the rest of the country was eliminated.

"I'm worried about them!" she said as we both realized we could be stranded here for days or even weeks. "And I can't wait and do nothing!" Much closer to home than I was, she decided to rent a car and make the drive north alone. She mapped out her route to circumvent all the major areas around New York and set off two days later. Still waiting to hear about any rescheduled flights, I was now alone in the hotel where I'd been staying since my arrival on September 10.

I watched interminable newscasts and worried constantly about the status of my own two families in California. Daily phone calls assured me that everyone in our families was fine. None of them thought I'd be safe driving alone back to California, so I waited until I was finally able to schedule a flight home on Sunday.

Unlike the trip from Raleigh to Wilmington on September 9, the drive back to Raleigh to return the car and fly back to Sacramento was entirely uneventful. Although the immediate emergency had ended, few people were on the roads, and the airport seemed hushed and almost silent, although I'm sure all of us flying home or wherever we had to be that Sunday were as worried about safety as I was. The tragedies of that horrific Tuesday morning continued to unfold, and life as I knew it would never be the same.

I'd spent most of my adult years on the West Coast, so the last place I wanted to be was on the East Coast. My childhood and early adulthood in New York City had provided many happy memories, but the tragedy of 9/11 would always cloud them. I never suspected that, in two short years, the life I now led would turn upside down, that I'd be leaving California for good and be heading back to the East Coast to live out the rest of my life in Florida.

Chapter Twenty-Two

"YOU WANT TO GO *WHERE?*"

JUST WHEN LIFE returned to near normal, I was blindsided again. My husband John, sixty-one and due to retire the next year, announced that he had decided where we would go when he turned sixty-two. He had talked about several options during the past two years, all near California where all our children lived, so I was astonished with this choice: we would be going to Merritt Island, Florida, not because it was the best of all options but because his younger sister Janet lived there. She talked him into moving there, and he set out to do just that.

I didn't just stand there and say nothing. "But what if I don't want to go? I'll miss my kids, as much as you'll miss yours, and all my friends are here. You won't be working, but I still have a career, and I finally have a job I love. Why would I want to leave?"

"I don't care about *any* of that. I'm going to Florida. With you or without you, I'm going to Florida," he said. No discussion necessary.

He had been in California for almost fifty years and was absolutely set against retiring there. I was finally in a nursing position that was a perfect fit for me and not ready to leave for Florida where I had no family or friends, but there was no talking him out of it. We were twenty-two years into a second marriage that had barely survived, but I hadn't yet given up on it. Even though I wasn't sure the move was the best plan for us and was doubtful we'd survive as a couple so far away from both California families, I reluctantly agreed to go along with it.

By mid-2002, he had made several trips to Florida, had found land in Merritt Island upon which to build a house, and contracted with a builder to put his dream home together, just five miles away from his sister and her family.

Because so many nurses with whom I worked in my facility had been hired as travel nurses from Florida, I knew what awaited me there. I was only sixty, physically and mentally fit, with many more years ahead of me in my career. Moving to Florida would mean higher patient-to-nurse ratios than were the norm in California and salaries less than half of what I currently earned.

"I won't be working," John said when I mentioned the lower salaries and those higher patient-to-nurse ratios. "It's not my problem." Despite those two issues and God only knew what else awaited me there, I was in this marriage for the long haul. I would go, but more and more reluctantly I faced the day that I would leave for Florida.

It didn't make it any easier when colleagues and friends asked, "You're going to leave us and live on an island in Florida?" It was as unbelievable as that, and each day that I spent as Administrative Supervisor became more bittersweet. I loved the challenges I faced in that position and knew I would miss all of them when I could no longer be there.

One of those challenges included three simultaneous Code Blue events one night when I'd just started my shift. The Administrative Supervisor was required to be present at all Code Blues to assist and coordinate what was needed for the staff, physicians, consultants, and families, carry out the necessary moves to ICU or CCU, and do all the other tasks so essential in these tense and often tragic situations. That night, two of the three patients survived and made it safely to Critical Care. The third, the elderly father of one of our Emergency Department physicians, was too critically ill to survive his crisis.

On another night, in two separate medical and surgical units in that facility, two patients deteriorated at the same time. In order to preclude calling simultaneous Code Blues in their non-monitored areas, I moved one to ICU and the other to CCU before their physicians, who hadn't yet responded to my calls, provided orders to do so. It impacted the staff in ICU and CCU, but they stepped up, handled both emergencies as efficiently as they always did, and both patients survived.

The Administrative Supervisor role was anything but static and left little time for the completion of necessary paperwork. More often than not, I ranged all over the building heading off problems, dealing with the ones that arose, and accomplishing the impossible job of keeping everyone safe. On one of those unforgettable nights, we handled case after case of Caesarean section emergencies that affected both the Obstetrics and Surgical services. C-Sections were usually performed in the Obstetrics Operating Room downstairs, but that night we had to utilize the main Operating Rooms on the second floor as well.

"I realize you need to keep one Operating Room available for emergency surgeries," I told the Emergency Department director, who had initially balked at freeing up that room when back-to-back C-Section patients began to overwhelm the Operating Room in Obstetrics. "But this is an emergency. We can't accommodate them all right now in OB."

I also spent hours negotiating with attending surgeons to free up two of the other OR suites to accommodate the cases that couldn't be handled in OB, then helped roll those patients, in their beds, up to the surgical suites on the second floor. That night we had ten obstetric emergencies that required Caesarean sections, and all ten mothers and babies did very well.

Our medical center was not a designated Neonatal Intensive Care facility, so one night we were on high alert for a potential premature multiple birth delivery of triplets to a young woman in her thirty-fourth week. Coordinating with Surgery, Obstetrics, and Newborn Nursery staff, we were able to handle this emergency as well. The mother did fine, and all three babies were in surprisingly good shape, despite their early arrival. They were rushed to the sister hospital's Neonatal Intensive Care Unit in Sacramento for monitoring and treatment. This was another happy memory I'd take with me when I left.

During my travels around the units on those shifts I knew I would profoundly miss, I often encountered people I'd met or known either in my professional role or in my private life. One night as I made rounds in all the units, I noticed the name of one of the professors with whom I'd studied years before at California State University. Not sure he was the same man, I stopped in to say hello, and his surprise was as profound as mine.

"So, you really are a nurse!" he laughed. "And call me Ron. A lot of years have passed since Cal State, and, now that I'm retired, nobody calls me Professor. I remember that last time I saw you. Bowling, wasn't it?"

"Birdcage Lanes." I smiled. "And that was years ago, after I finished at Cal State."

He had headed the Russian Language Studies Department. I audited his class of first-year Russian students during the 1974-1975 academic year at CSU Sacramento, my last one there. Completing my Master's in Creative Writing, I had also been taking an elective Russian History class with his colleague in the History Department. Both were excellent teachers. My Liberal Arts education had been enriched because of them.

I hadn't seen Professor Grainger again until the early 1980s while bowling in the same league at Birdcage Lanes in North Sacramento. And now, in 2002, I could see he had changed very little. Several years older than I, he had retired from the university, was living in this community near the medical center, and, like me, was reluctantly facing a move to Florida in the next few months.

He would be in Cocoa, not far from my new home in Merritt Island, and I promised to look him up when I finally made the move a year later. I didn't know that the next time we met would be the last time, or that it would be in my professional role at the medical center in Titusville, charge nurse to patient, as he lay dying from lung cancer with multiple sites in his brain and lungs.

At home in Sacramento, plans for the move to Florida moved inexorably forward. Our new home was being built in Merritt Island, our home in Sacramento had been sold in one day, and my husband had decided to temporarily move in with his daughter and her family. I had arranged for a room in the home of one of my nursing colleagues near the medical center.

Although I would have been paying the rent for us, my husband had flatly rejected the idea of an apartment together because he preferred to live with his daughter and her family from January to May, when he was due to retire. I didn't want to burden his family with an additional roomer, one who was working in two complex night positions, the first in Roseville and the second in Sacramento. I also needed that option to think clearly about the move to Florida that would so radically change my life. Moving in with my colleague seemed the best option at the time, but within a few months I started to regret it.

Chapter Twenty-Three

THE BEGINNING OF THE END–AND THE END OF THE BEGINNING

BETWEEN JANUARY AND November 2003, I experienced some of the most memorable moments of my nursing career, but the impending move to Florida now colored everything.

I continued the dual roles of Administrative Supervisor and per diem Emergency nurse, worked three weeks out of four in California, then spent the fourth one in Florida. I needed the time there to decide if I really wanted to make the move and, in case I did, to prepare our new home for the potential arrival in November. It would be our first new home together, and my goal was to make it as comfortable and livable as possible.

The house was finished and ready for occupancy by mid-May, the same month John retired. While he made the major decisions about the house itself, I made most of the ones about how to furnish and decorate it.

My mother's legacy to me provided sufficient funds for that six-month project, so I set to work on those week-long visits making our new home beautiful and comfortable for both of us. If I couldn't be entirely happy about the move, I could be happy about the home where we would live out the rest of our lives.

The most disrupting aspect of that move was constant interference from my husband's sister. Living less than five miles away, she inserted herself into all aspects of planning and building the house. This wasn't a problem for John, who had deferred to her all his life, but it became a huge problem for us, as he learned a week after he moved to Florida in May, and the furniture from our home in California was delivered.

I had asked him to wait until my next trip before moving all the furniture into the house so we could decide together where it should be placed. He didn't want the furniture I'd brought to the marriage twenty-three years before, but he knew we needed everything from the old house to furnish our new one. True to form, he decided to do as he pleased with the furniture and then asked his sister to help him move all of it into the house.

"This is our house, damn it! Not hers!" I said when he reluctantly admitted it. "Sister or not, you should never have asked her to help you, and she should never have agreed to do it!"

But when he confessed about the furniture, he also said, "I guess I'd better tell you about the rats."

"What rats?"

"On the trip from California to Florida, the moving van picked up a family of rats that made their home in the furniture the movers had put into the new garage. So . . . when we . . . the day we moved the furniture into the house, the rats moved right along with it, and . . .".

"And?"

" . . . destroyed most of the newly installed wiring. Our builder wasn't happy and made us move all that furniture back into the garage until the wiring had been replaced and the rats were gone."

"Is there anything else you've forgotten to tell me?"

He denied it, but hadn't told me the most important thing. I wouldn't know about it until months later as I continued the trips from Sacramento to Central Florida, waiting for the other shoe to drop.

Back in California, renting a room in the home of a nursing colleague with whom I still worked became just one more major problem. Leona was several years older than I and rigid with rules about my presence in her home, like when I ate, what I placed in my room, or when I was permitted to shower. As demanding and unbending as my husband, she made those eight months from February through September almost unbearable. I put up with her as long as possible because of our work together and her reliance on the rent I paid her.

In October, I'd finally had enough. "I'm barely hanging on. These Florida trips are always an ordeal. I'm exhausted when I get there and exhausted when I get back. No matter how quiet I am and how much I try not to be a nuisance, you're not happy with anything I do. You knew my schedule when you offered me a room here; you accept the rent I pay you, but you've never made me feel welcome. I'm not sure I even want to stay."

After that, she barely spoke to me. I was fortunate to find a residential hotel that accepted me for that last month in California. I'd already shipped most of my clothing and belongings to Florida, so I had just one large carton and several suitcases to deal with for those final days before I left.

That week, John came back from Florida for my final farewell celebration at the same medical center from which he'd retired six months before. When he arrived, he announced that he would make the drive back to Florida in my car, I would fly alone to Florida, and his sister Janet, who had flown to California with him, would make the cross-country car trip in my place. Added to the already tense atmosphere between us since my last trip to Florida in October, I almost decided right then to give up and not make the move at all.

On that October trip, I had gone into the library in Merritt Island one morning to apply for a library card. I had always had a library card anywhere I had lived. No matter how unbearable things could get, I would always have a book to read.

"I'm so sorry," the librarian told me when I turned in the application. "You must be a resident of the county to obtain a library card."

"But I am a resident—or soon will be. I'm moving to our new home here in November."

"You have to be a legal resident. I looked up your new address on the county records, and your name isn't listed. The only one listed as property owner is John."

I was stunned to learn that the title to the new house and the land it stood on had been filed in his name only. I would be moving to an entirely new part of the country with no family and no friends to fall back on, to a home that wasn't legally mine, to a new job in nursing not yet verified, and I couldn't even get a library card!

John agreed to take care of the property issue and my resident status before I made the move in November, but now he had altered my travel plans. I would be flying alone to Florida on Sunday. In addition, he informed me that his daughter and her family would be arriving the following Wednesday for Thanksgiving and staying through the weekend.

"Did you even think to ask if I'd be ready to have company for five days? I'll barely have time to unpack!"

Like most of his decisions, John made this one without me. I had no choice but to make the most of it. I loved his daughter and her family and would be happy to see all of them, but, in preparing for their visit, I would have no time to settle into my new home.

With so many things against the move and with so many more problems to come, I'd have been far better off to stay in California. But I'd never backed down from anything, including anything as painful as this move had already turned out to be. I boarded the plane in Sacramento on that Sunday morning before Thanksgiving, said goodbye to the life I'd made for myself on the West Coast for forty years, and braced myself for whatever was yet to come.

Chapter Twenty-Four

A NEW LIFE FOR THE OLD

IF 2003 WAS one of the worst years of my life, 2004 ran a close second. I knew there had to be some sense in giving up that old life for the new one. I also knew that the best way to accomplish it was to reinvent myself all over again. But not even that task looked promising as Christmas and New Year's Day came and went, and I hadn't yet heard if my application for the position of Emergency Department Assistant Nurse Manager had been accepted.

The November interview with both current Emergency Department Assistant Nurse Managers had gone well. They liked me and my work history, said they would recommend me to their nurse manager, and told me they would be in touch by the end of the month. I never heard from them again but learned from Human Resources the first week in January that their Emergency Department Nurse Manager had not accepted my application. More puzzling still, I was offered instead the Assistant Nurse Manager position in Medical Oncology, for which I hadn't applied and for which I wasn't prepared. In all my past nursing experiences, I hadn't once considered oncology, but the Director there apparently thought I would be a perfect fit for the position and snapped me up when the one in the Emergency Department disappeared.

After the past two months of reluctant retirement, determined to make the best of what would soon become an extremely bad situation, I accepted the new offer. My salary would be less than half of what I'd earned in California, I would be in a middle-management position in a specialty in which I had never worked, and I'd be dealing with staff and senior management personnel that I didn't know. I would require more determination and patience than ever before. As it turned out, it was better that I didn't know exactly what that would mean.

It probably wasn't an omen, but on the day that I started my new role, in a facility that had been open only since late 2003, the prior hospital building set for demolition that day tumbled down seamlessly, straight across the parking lot from the new one where I had just begun orientation. I wondered if I, like that old building, would finally collapse under the weight of all my new and overwhelming nursing challenges.

From the outset, they seemed exactly that. As Assistant Nurse Manager on the ten-hour night shift, I'd be in charge of the forty-two-bed unit that had single and double patient rooms in the North, West, and South Wings. I'd always have my own team of eight to nine patients as well as overall management of the entire unit, just one patient care technician to assist with the physical care of all the patients, and one secretary to do admission orders and paperwork for all the units in the hospital. To make matters worse, I'd be required to work with an incomprehensible computerized medical records system when, for me, computers had always been difficult to understand and comfortably utilize.

Oncology patients on the North Wing required chemotherapy and all the specialized programs inherent in their care. Not having studied oncology in my lengthy career, I needed to get up to speed as quickly as possible. The other patients in the unit were medical and gerontology patients who had come to Florida to enjoy their retirement. Most of them also required cardiac monitoring. This wasn't a problem for me, with all my prior Emergency and Critical Care assignments. It was a problem there because they were monitored in a room one floor below ours. With no monitors on our floor, there was no way for me or my staff to actually observe changes in their cardiac status. I thought that was dangerous and said so, which didn't endear me to the nursing leaders.

I also became concerned about the need to closely monitor our patients with pulmonary diagnoses. Pulse oximetry, assessing oxygen saturation by attaching a sensor to a patient's finger and extrapolating oxygen content via capillary blood flow, had already been utilized for years in California. NASA scientists had developed it to monitor astronauts, and I was amazed it wasn't in use in this hospital as a component of all vital signs.

"That's not a nursing responsibility," the Respiratory Therapy manager told me when I asked about it.

"How can it not be? It should be a component of all the vital signs we monitor, especially with so many of our patients on multiple cardiac, respiratory, and pain medications." After I continued voicing my concerns to the Respiratory Therapy Department and Nursing Administration, it did eventually become common practice.

This was a new facility with all the latest equipment, but such simple things as oxygen and suction gauges on the wall units in every room weren't available and never became available, despite the many times I requested them in my two years in the Assistant Nurse Manager position.

Besides not monitoring cardiac patients where we could actually observe the cardiac rhythms, we were constantly understaffed and also required to adhere to a protocol by which all patients in the ED who required enemas until clear were sent to our floor to receive them.

"You can't be serious!" I told the night shift Administrative Supervisor the first time she informed me about it. "Nowhere in any Emergency Departments I've ever worked have patients been sent to Inpatient areas for something that could be done in ED Holding! It means having to move them from Outpatient to Inpatient status and back to Outpatient status again, not to mention stress on the patients and the staff."

It made absolutely no sense, but the practice continued as long as I worked there. Because our one patient care technician was assigned to most of the patients on the unit, I assumed the role of Enema Queen. I provided the enemas and ensured that those patients who required them didn't have comorbidities that the ED nurses failed to report before sending them up to us. Giving enemas to already compromised cardiac or neurological patients was always a potential danger due to possible fluid overload from enema solutions.

For staff who had worked only in this facility and had limited experience with the kind of quality nursing care provided in more professionally managed institutions, none of these practices seemed at all unusual. I knew better and raised questions about all of them to physicians and Nursing Administration, but nothing changed while I worked there.

Frustrated and not sure I'd survive this new role, I knew I wouldn't at the end of the summer of 2004 when the Space Coast of Central Florida was struck by not one but four major hurricanes, and I was caught in the middle of all of them.

Chapter Twenty-Five

STORMY WEATHER

METEOROLOGISTS CALLED IT the Summer of Storms, the worst cluster of deadly storms to strike the Space Coast of Central Florida in more than a hundred years. Initially a tropical storm, Charlie became the first major hurricane at the end of the summer of 2004. Because it had had little impact on our new home five miles south of the Kennedy Space Center, John and I were lulled into believing we wouldn't be touched.

But Labor Day Weekend changed everything. What started as simply a tropical storm in the Caribbean morphed into a monster named Frances who soon destroyed all the complacency that anyone had ever felt about the invulnerability of the Kennedy Space Center.

For four days and nights, Hurricane Frances became my personal nightmare. Before she even made landfall, I was twenty-five miles to the north, a member of my unit on the fifth floor of the hospital in Titusville. Once I crossed the bridge linking Merritt Island to the mainland, there was no turning back, since all the bridges had been closed once the winds reached fifty miles per hour.

It was early afternoon that Friday when I left home with my little rolling suitcase and headed north. I'd packed the bare minimum of what I thought I'd need for however long it took to survive Frances, still hovering off the coast at the southern end of Brevard County. Just to be safe, I'd included a spare set of uniform scrubs and several more shirts, in case I ever had an opportunity to change them.

The sky, a ghastly gunmetal gray, loomed overhead as I drove down State Route 3, headed across the Causeway and into the city of Titusville. This northern end of Brevard County was strangely silent, with little traffic on US 1, and tiny American flags on poles on both sides of the highway waving bravely in the wind. I made it safely, and still dry, to the staff parking lot at the south end of the medical center complex before the rain that had been threatening all day fell straight down, a harbinger of the deluge we'd be facing in the days and nights to come.

For whatever reason Administration made the ruling, physicians and their families, along with the staff assigned to work that weekend, would all be staying in the allotted space usually reserved for patients. None of us were permitted to bring our own families to the medical center, and those of us assigned to A Team had to make do with the rooms not already taken over by the physicians and their families. There were six of us in a single patient room on the South Wing of our fifth floor, with only one bathroom, two beds, and one cot allotted to us as we rotated in and out on day and night shifts.

On that first day, it was barely controlled chaos. As Assistant Nurse Manager, I was assigned to patient care in the third floor Surgical Unit, in rooms on the East and North Wings. The rain continued to pour, but the hurricane itself had not yet made landfall by the time the night shift began at 7 p.m. Awake all day and not about to get any sleep that night, I was as anxious as everyone else as, one by one, we lost contact with all the area television stations and had to depend upon local radio stations still transmitting to provide information about the storm's progress.

Hurricane Frances finally made landfall a few minutes after midnight at Sebastian Inlet far south on the Treasure Coast. Now we were in for monsoon rains that continued unabated from late in the afternoon on Friday until early afternoon on Monday.

Like most of us stranded there that holiday weekend, concerned about our families at home, I worried constantly about my husband, alone with no electricity and no telephone once his cell phone lost its last charge. Fortunately, I had patient care and staffing issues to occupy me, so time passed more quickly, but, like my stranded colleagues, I wished that Administration had permitted us to have our own families there with us. The constant roar of the storm and the noise of generator power we were under added to our stress. None of us had more than a few hours of sleep at a time. As Saturday rolled into Sunday and there seemed to be no end in sight to our long and enforced lockdown, tempers frayed and our patience with the ordeal wore extremely thin.

That Sunday morning, the Emergency Department Director who had refused to hire me suffered a public meltdown and had to be escorted out of the lobby where she had begun to babble and cry out hysterically. "What's going on with her?" I asked one of my Assistant Nurse Manager colleagues from the Surgical unit.

She shrugged and reluctantly told me, "Rumors about drinking. It's been a problem, and she has been counseled, but this hurricane has been too much for her. I guess being trapped here for who knows how long and not being able to get to her alcohol has been too much."

That's probably why I wasn't offered that position in Emergency. That Director could count on her present staff and colleagues to protect her, but an outsider with many more years in Emergency nursing would probably assess her problem instantly and want it resolved. While I empathized with her dilemma, I was happy I hadn't been offered the position in the Emergency Department after all.

As that long day wore on, we remained under generator power with dim to no lighting and rapidly diminishing food supplies, due to the added need to feed physicians and their families as well as all the staff enduring the lockdown.

The eye of the hurricane eventually moved on by Sunday evening, and by early Monday morning we began making plans for the arrival of the B Team. I still hadn't made contact with John and had no idea if the bridge across the Intercoastal Waterway that linked Titusville with Merritt Island would be open. But, by late afternoon, beyond exhausted and not about to spend any more time there, I left the medical center and headed south down US 1. As I headed home, all the bridges were open, but I didn't know if anything was left of the new house we'd lived in for a little over a year. Not for the first time, I wondered what we were doing in Florida and if we would have to start all over again.

Chapter Twenty-Six

IVAN AND JEAN

NO SOONER HAD we survived Hurricanes Charlie and Frances, Ivan became the third great storm to savage Florida that summer. Right on his heels came Jean, and although I was off duty during Ivan, I was back on the job with Jean.

This time, I was the only member of my unit's management team to be on-site. Julie, the day shift Assistant Nurse Manager, was designated for B Team cleanup duties. Our Manager, Moira, in discussions with the Nursing Administrator over undisclosed personal issues, declined to report to work during Jean. Ready or not, I took her place at the numerous planning sessions during the two days and nights I was there.

Once again, there would be no telephone contact with John. This time, however, there were no physicians or their families to take over most of the space allotted for staff requiring sleep between shifts, and there was enough food for all of us in lockdown.

It should have been an easy two days since we had so recently been through it on Labor Day weekend with Frances. But members of my staff took this storm to act out their many frustrations long ignored by Nursing Administration. These included the continuing lack of equipment, poor staffing, and ongoing problems with one of our patient care techs, who always seemed to be missing when needed, was always resentful when ordered back to work, and always scarier than hell when counseled.

"Where I go and what I do are none of your damn business!" she smirked as I stopped her on the way back from wherever she'd been for the past hour, the second time she'd gone missing that night.

"I think it is. You know I'll report it, and I'll keep reporting it until the Nursing Director does something about it!" Annoyed that no one in authority had yet taken action, I stared her down until she stalked away.

I went back to my home on Merritt Island after those two days and nights, exhausted but gratified that upper-level management had noticed and commended my courage under fire throughout this latest hurricane. They had no idea how close I'd been to losing it before Hurricane Jean headed toward Georgia, and we finally got back to normal.

That summer of storms had been so much more than I'd bargained for when I accepted the position of Assistant Nurse Manager earlier that year. By September, I wasn't sure I wanted to remain in that unit any longer, tilting at windmills and not accepted by management or staff who saw me as the know-it-all outsider from California.

That all changed for the better one night when one of those windmills, an attending physician who invariably treated the nursing staff with open hostility, struck my last nerve when he refused to provide a medication order for a dying patient. In desperation, one of my night shift staff nurses, insulted much too frequently in her calls to this physician, begged me to call him after she'd done all she could to comfort this patient and her family. They had already asked the physician for another, more potent medication to alleviate her pain, but he had not written the order or called it in to the unit after he left that evening.

"Just what qualifications do you have to tell me what my patient needs?" He was as curt and dismissive with me as he had been with my staff member. This was about a patient who needed him, not about my qualifications to request the medication. I and my entire staff had had enough of his bullying.

"Enough to know that when a patient needs her physician, he takes care of her."

I should have told him that, after forty-two years in nursing, I had more experience with patients than he had ever had. I should have calmly repeated my request for the medication order, but he had to have the last word.

"I'll be the one to determine what my patient does or does not need. Do not call me again!" he told me.

I'd finally had enough. "Then just do your job! You're no damned doctor. You're an asshole!" I hung up on him before he could say another word. When he called back and demanded to speak to the nurse in charge, I said, "You're speaking to her!" and hung up on him again.

As expected, he didn't hesitate to report me to the Administrative Supervisor, so I assumed that the Nursing Director would hand me my walking papers before I left the hospital the next morning. The staff on the unit were amazed and grateful for what I'd done, and so were the Director and Assistant Director of Nursing when I met with them. "Someone should have done that a long time ago," they told me, smiling. They couldn't believe anyone would take him on and were really appreciative that I had. Their only request was for me to write an apology—but not to him—for my language. "Damned" and "asshole" were not exactly proper terms to use when addressing our not-so-esteemed physicians.

The upside to all of this was better acceptance by my nursing peers, since I'd taken a chance and crawled out on a pretty shaky limb for them. More importantly, both the Nursing Director and the Medical Chief of Staff recognized that something had to be done to improve physician/nurse relationships. Over the objections of those physicians most notorious for harassing nurses in that facility, the Medical Chief of Staff consulted with a physician who specialized in conflict resolution between all healthcare professionals. That component of problems that had dogged me since accepting the Assistant Nurse Manager position changed for the better. But there were still others.

Those problems included continued understaffing, continued transfers of patients from the Emergency Department for enemas, and another far more serious patient care issue: an alarming increase in episodes of adverse reactions to Hydromorphone. Also known as known as Dilaudid, Hydromorphone was a narcotic three to four times more potent than morphine. Its analgesic effect was achieved at 0.5 to 1.0 milligrams, but patients required closer monitoring if provided with higher doses or if they received other potentially lethal medications. This was the medication my husband had received after his lithotripsy years before in California and the one for which he'd needed to be admitted for closer observation.

One night in this medical center in Florida, one of my staff came running to get me because she hadn't been able to awaken her patient after she had medicated her for back pain several hours earlier.

"What did you give her?" I asked after I checked the patient who was neither moving nor breathing.

"What was ordered. Dilaudid."

My heart sank. This patient had been stone-cold dead for hours. "What dose?"

"Her doctor ordered two milligrams."

"And she received all of it?"

"Yes."

"And you checked her vital signs afterward?"

"An hour after I gave it. At midnight. And there had been no change."

As it turned out, the patient had been gravely ill, and because she wasn't one of the patients for whom telemetry had been ordered, she simply died, pain free. Dilaudid had been a factor but not the primary cause of her death. In recent months, in another area of the hospital, two other patients had received Dilaudid, had not been closely monitored, and one had also died.

This incident became a reminder for all of us to more closely observe patients who received that narcotic. Then I found myself in hot water with Nursing Administration once more for a different reason. "Why didn't you call a Code Blue when you found her?" the Administrative Supervisor asked me.

"Because there was no blood pressure or breath sounds, and it had been at least two hours since she'd been checked. Calling a Code would have been a waste of time for that already overburdened staff."

"But the policy states . . ."

"Code Blues are to resuscitate patients who can be resuscitated, damn it! Not patients who are already going into rigor." Nursing Administration supported me on that decision, but, once more, I had to apologize for my language. "Damn" was not a word I should have used with my supervisor.

That fall, after an especially wet summer, standing water accumulating on the flat rooftop of what was essentially still a new facility had become a concern for Plant Operations. One night, it became a major concern for me as well. Nothing had been said about a leak problem during shift report, but, several hours later, busy with my own team of eight patients on the West Wing and staffing issues on the South Wing, I received a frantic call from the nurse assigned to the North Wing. "Oh, my God! You've got to get down here!" She was usually one of the most unflappable RNs on staff. Just hearing her voice now made my heart lurch in my chest. It had to be bad if she was calling for help.

"Which room?"

"Five forty-nine. And hurry!"

Heart racing, I ran from the far end of the West Wing, down the long hallway in the North Wing, and stopped at the last room on the left. The ceiling in Room 549 had collapsed over the bed of the patient and onto the cot where his family member had been resting. Startled out of sleep, she jumped up when the wet tile and water struck her and fell in the water now covering the floor. The patient, an elderly man diagnosed with lymphoma, managed to avoid the falling water and tile, but, in trying to help his family member, began experiencing severe chest pain.

There was no time to waste. I assisted his nurse in getting both of them to safety and out of that room where, at any moment, more water and tiles could fall. I knew the same thing could also happen in other rooms on that wing. As soon as I could get help for the injured woman and an EKG for the man with chest pain, I'd handle that and all the other possibly endangered patients.

I then called the Administrative Supervisor and Plant Operations Manager, and while I waited for them to call back, ordered a stat EKG for the man, and helped the woman onto a stretcher for her transfer down to the ED. Everything was handled by the time the Plant Operations Manager and Administrative Supervisor arrived. While the Manager checked all the other rooms for safety issues, and the Supervisor arranged a transfer to Coronary Care for the man, now diagnosed with an acute myocardial infarction (MI), I went back my patients on the West Wing.

The lymphoma patent survived his MI and the family member, sister of his elderly wife who had died just months before, did well after surgery for the hip she'd fractured in her fall. This sentinel event, one in which a patient suffers death, permanent harm, or severe temporary harm, should have been reported right away to the Risk Manager. When I'd asked the Supervisor to do so, she had dithered and dallied and said it wasn't my responsibility to tell her what to do. This was the same woman who had reported me after my altercation with the arrogant physician I'd put in his place and who insisted I should have called a Code Blue on a patient dead for hours. When I learned that she waited until morning to notify Risk Management about the event, I decided not to say anything to the Director of Nursing. That would be her problem, and, by now, I recognized a lost cause when I saw it.

Because of the continuing inability of the department manager to fulfill all her duties due to personal reasons, I was delegated to take over the scheduling of ancillary and nursing staff for the unit, a thankless job even in the best of times. If one staff member was happy with her schedule, another was not, and keeping the uneasy peace between warring factions was more than I'd expected to be doing.

By the fall of 2006, I was ready to look for a position in a facility as far away as I could get from the one in which I'd been working. What had saved me for the past two years was attending the writers' conferences in Hawaii and renewing my interest in finally writing the medical-legal mystery I'd started, which included the insanity of my nursing roles in Florida, the drama of the hurricanes that had made history, and most of the main characters in the prequel, *Past Believing*.

Plans to finish it, write a second draft, and pursue a publisher had to be placed on hold, however, with all the major changes occurring in my role as Assistant Nurse Manager during those last momentous months in 2006. Nursing had always been my primary passion, and writing again took second place to the ongoing drama on the fifth floor in that medical center in North Brevard County.

Unable to resolve her personal/professional conflicts, the manager finally resigned, and the former Assistant Director of Nursing/ Director of Nursing Operations took her place. It wasn't the best choice since she had no support from the unit staff and had been one of the major sources of unrest for them. For her part, this had been a major step down in status, and she had no idea how to resolve any of the problems facing her as the Director of the unit. Among them was her anger at my refusal to fire one of the staff nurses, not because her work was an issue—she was an excellent bedside nurse—but because of her frequent challenges to Administration over poor staffing and patient safety. The new Director was also unhappy over my refusal to fire one of the patient care technicians, also excellent with patients, just because she didn't like his somewhat quirky personality.

That fall, after a less than acceptable annual evaluation from the new manager, which overlooked all the efforts I'd made to keep the patients safe and the unit together, I'd finally had enough. I decided to look for positions as far away as Orlando when an opportunity I had never before considered presented itself.

Until then, oncology had been provided on the North Wing of my unit, with the nurses providing in-house chemotherapy to those patients starting initial and occasional subsequent rounds of chemotherapy. There had been no department head, per se, until that fall when a Master's-prepared Nurse Practitioner became Director. Although oncology patients had been cared for in the unit, they, like numerous oncology patients in Brevard County, had always been referred to Moffitt, the prestigious oncology center in Tampa. With the newly designated Oncology Department and Director on board, a strong professional partnership was established.

I'd been applying for Emergency Department positions in Orlando, since ED had always been one of my favorite assignments, when a newly created position involving genomic research became available at my current facility. It required the development of a new research program between our hospital and the cancer center in Tampa. Not sure I could do it or even if Research was what I wanted, I applied for the position before I left for vacation in California, hoping that, after the past two years, this position would be a better fit for me.

Chapter Twenty-Seven

DIVING INTO TOTAL CANCER CARE

IT TOOK AN enormous leap of faith to accept the research role in Total Cancer Care. In all my years in nursing, I'd never considered oncology. Although I had been Assistant Manager on a Medical Oncology unit for the past two years and passed the rigorous chemotherapy course the year before, I'd had little to do with the oncology end of it. But I had already survived two terrifying hurricane seasons and two tempestuous years in my current role, so I thought, *Why not give it a try?*

Since accepting her new position as Oncology Director, Gisela Bach had investigated several programs that would enhance our own. Total Cancer Care was a perfect fit for us. Gisela confessed to me a few months later that she had felt intimidated by my education and experience when she'd read my résumé. That wasn't a problem for me then since it had happened before with other nursing colleagues, but it would become one the longer I worked with her. Thankfully, I didn't know it at the time.

As she explained when she offered me the position, "You'll be taking over two research programs that deal with cancer prevention, but you'll be primary researcher in Total Cancer Care. That means you'll be working with Surgery and Pathology physicians and staff in our facility as well as the entire research team in Tampa. Are you ready to take that on?"

"Definitely!"

"You'll need an office, but there's nothing available on this floor, so I'll check for one on Third. It's for surgical and post-surgical patients, so you'll be close to the ones enrolled in Total Cancer Care."

I had no clear idea of the enormity of Total Cancer Care and all it would entail, but, at sixty-four and nowhere near retirement, I accepted this latest challenge, which lasted from January 2006 through late November 2007. In doing so, I embarked on one of the most unforgettable and painful professional journeys I'd ever taken, but I wouldn't regret one memorable moment of it.

I began by developing my oncology skills and learning the intricacies of cancer care in the most prestigious cancer research and treatment center in the state. That also meant preparing to take the Oncology Nurse Certification Exam in November. Determined to pass the exam on the first attempt, I went online every day at work and at home on the weekends, immersing myself in all the modalities of oncology care. My experiences with patients during the past forty years helped immeasurably, but passing that exam in an entirely different nursing specialty wouldn't be easy.

This is not like the Bar Exam! I had to remind myself. *I know patient care, and I have a lot more invested in nursing than I ever had in Law. I can do this!*

It took from January until May to complete all the preparations for the Total Cancer Care Program, incorporating multiple meetings, exhausting trips back and forth to Tampa, and then innumerable dry runs with actual patients to enroll them in the program. The basic premise of Total Cancer Care was to enroll already diagnosed or soon to be diagnosed patients into the program by completing inclusion data on computer tablets supplied by the Cancer Center. They were connected to Tampa by the proprietary statewide network, which I didn't completely understand, but, no longer a novice with computer technology, I accepted the challenge and jumped right in. To my surprise, I actually started to enjoy it.

I would be alerted about a possible enrollee by either the oncologist or the surgeon due to conduct a biopsy. As soon as possible, I would interview the patient, explain the process, and enroll him or her into Total Cancer Care. Then I would go to the Operating Room with the patient, wait in my minilab at the far end of the surgical suite for the excised tissue to be delivered, then take it down to Pathology on the first floor. Once the tissue was processed, I would return the tissue, packed and sealed, to my lab in the OR, label it, and place it into one of the liquid nitrogen containers, where it would remain until sent to the research center in Tampa.

It took enormous energy to coordinate all aspects of the program, endure long waits for excised tissue, and, more importantly, convince patients and their families that this research project, based on the genomics of cancer diagnosis and treatment, would be invaluable in the planning and institution of their individual courses of treatment.

In addition to the constant pressure to find and enroll as many patients as possible—not easy in this non-urban setting in the north end of Brevard County—I was also involved in patient care follow-up and dealing with the constantly critical Gisela Bach. Driven by her own personal agenda, she made it clear she was in charge and that I worked *for* her, not with her. I was on my own, and although Total Cancer Care became a success for our facility, she resented anyone who thanked me for the hard work I carried out for our facility and the Cancer Center in Tampa. Struggling to complete the requirements for her advanced degree in nursing and thwarted in her attempts to secure the directorship of the entire Medical-Oncology department, she focused her unhappiness on me during those twenty-two months, and, on the weekend after Thanksgiving, she found the perfect opportunity to make me leave.

I'd passed the Oncology Nurse Certification exam on the first attempt, completed the Breast Cancer Navigation program, and was one of the winners in our facility's contest to name new projects for our employees (a proposal for a Gone-But-Not-Forgotten Garden in memory of staff who had died) when I made the mistake that would cost me my position.

Gisela came to work that week, happily announcing to anyone who would listen that she would be undergoing a procedure to diagnose possible gallbladder pathology. I'd never heard of the procedure. Although I had had no interest in Gisela's personal life or healthcare problems, I was curious about that new procedure. Without thinking, I opened her file to check the correct terminology. I didn't find it, but I had opened the file, and those were the days when HIPPA (Hospital Privacy and Portability ACT) violations were closely monitored. By opening her file, I'd broken one of the rules and would pay dearly for it.

It had been a good week, with new patients enrolled in the Total Cancer Care program and an interview with a local news writer fascinated by the program in which our North Brevard County facility was involved. Although I'd asked the writer to focus on all of us involved in the Total Cancer Care project, she didn't mention Gisela or her Directorship of the Oncology Department, and I knew that would become a problem for me, who was in an already tenuous position.

The article came out on the last Friday in November, the same day I was called into a meeting with the Director of Personnel and two members of her department. As soon as I took that call, I knew that Gisela, whom I had actually informed about opening her file, had gone straight to Personnel.

There had been no malice in accessing her file, but she apparently saw it as an opportunity to force my resignation, and that's exactly what happened. The Personnel Director wasn't happy about the resignation since the incident had been minor and had no impact on Gisela personally or professionally, but Gisela had taken it straight to a good friend, one of the facility administrators, and that was that.

Thanks to the Personnel Director, who emphatically refused to have me escorted out of the building by Security, the standard demoralizing punishment levied in that facility, I was given the weekend to clear out my office and return the keys.

Once the shock wore off, and I had the weekend to leave the job behind physically and mentally, I realized everything happens for a reason, and that Gisela had actually done me a great favor. I had loved the challenges of initiating and carrying out the research project and my role in Total Cancer Care. I had also stretched and grown in more ways than I ever imagined, but dealing with Gisela day-to-day had become an ordeal, and I was happy to see the end of her. Little did I know that, in leaving that position and taking on a new one, I'd be jumping into another fire even more painful than the one I just left.

John shrugged when I'd told him about losing the research position and said simply, "I hope you manage to keep this one" when I told him about the second one. Once again, I wondered why I'd ever moved to Florida and why I ever imagined the move would bring us closer together.

Chapter Twenty-Eight

INTO THE FIRE– AGAIN

LESS THAN A week after losing the position with Gisela Bach, I found another one with the Medical Director of the research program I'd just left. He knew my work ethic and was surprisingly laid back during my interview when I admitted I'd broken that HIPPA privacy rule in opening Gisela's file.

"It's nothing that warrants a dismissal," he'd said, but he had his own agenda. His new oncology practice facility would be completed within the next few months. His staff and medical colleagues knew he would need a Nurse Navigator. I was pleased that he had chosen me, but in the relief of finding a new way to continue caring for cancer patients and their families, I failed to ignore another caveat I had learned all too well: "Be careful what you wish for."

Although I may have hoped for a medical director who would remain encouraging and supportive and a navigation program that would meet all the patients' needs, I had to settle for a new state-of-the-art building in which to work, wonderful patients and families, and a position that constantly changed focus. The Medical Director had no real plans for the navigator role, but I soon learned he expected instant success in everything I attempted to accomplish for him.

The Oncology/Hematology practice consisted of four offices. The primary one was in the city in North Brevard where I had worked for

three years, with the others in Rockledge, Cocoa Beach, and Merritt
Island, the city where I'd lived since moving to Florida in 2003.

With no clear idea of what to do with me, the Medical Director
assigned me to the office building across the street from the actual
practice offices and treatment center only several miles from home.
From January until mid-March, I camped out in that large, open room
where the business side of the practice was carried out, scrunched
down in a low-to-the-floor desk that sent my right sciatic nerve into
constant and painful spasms. It wasn't until mid-March, in my own
office in the new medical complex in North Brevard, that the spasms
ended and I could walk without pain. I never told anyone about them.
The last thing I needed was to be seen as the same complainer who had
been a thorn in the side of nursing management at the medical center
two years before concentrating my goals on oncology.

This new position with the private oncology practice was initially
daunting as I learned the intricacies of the practice, tried to fit in comfortably with the business office staff, did my damnedest to understand
what the Medical Director expected of me and how to survive his
mercurial changes of mood when I didn't. I did meet with many of
the men and women working with pharmaceutical companies, hoping to sponsor dinner meetings once we moved into the new building
in March. I also succeeded in re-establishing several patient support
groups that hadn't met since November. In February, I learned that
the Total Cancer Care project with the Cancer Center in Tampa had
ended when my old nemesis, Gisela Bach, hadn't continued it or hired
anyone in my place.

The oncology practice moved into the new building in March, and
I kept busy by meeting new patients, setting up and presiding over
dinner meetings for the local physicians, and initiating and hosting
several more support groups that met in our large multi-purpose conference room. It was an exciting time, and everything we attempted
was a huge success.

We held an Opening of the New Building celebration that first

June, including what would become an annual art show supported by the national organization that promoted a competition for cancer survivors and their families. In our second year, one of our local artists placed first, and our Medical Director couldn't have been prouder. We held two successful Survivors' Summits those first two years, and patients and their families were grateful for how thoroughly we advocated for all of them.

By the middle of the third year, however, things started changing. Fewer new patients had been coming in due to the unexpected but imminent closure of so many of the programs at the Kennedy Space Center. In the past, many of our new patients had been referred from the Space Center and enrolled in our oncology program, thanks to one of their executives who'd been diagnosed with a rare cancer and treated successfully by our physicians.

That all started to change as many of the personnel working the Kennedy Space Center or who contracted with the multitude of programs supporting NASA at the Space Center began to retire and leave the area. The oncology practice Medical Director became irascible and not at all supportive of the Navigation program. He lost one research nurse and then another, and there was also talk of possible legal action taken by one of his partners who had also left the practice.

The Director became more and critical of me for my failure to entice new patients into the practice, which had never been one of my duties. In addition, he never agreed with my efforts to develop a ride-sharing program for patients who had no means to travel to our center for appointments or radiation treatments. That summer, he hired a new Administrator. Although we already had one, he hired this one intending to cut costs to the bone and rid himself of anyone and everyone who didn't totally agree with his philosophy.

My role as Advocate and Navigator had never been a direct financial benefit to the oncology practice, and because the decrease in new patients had continued, I was one of the first of the staff to be let go. It happened the first Friday in August, when the new Administrator called me into her office to inform me that the Advocate and Navigator position had been eliminated.

"And me as well? There is no other position available?"

I knew it but couldn't resist asking.

"You'll be paid until the end of the month, but there are no other employment options available for you here."

After all was said and done, I was relieved. It hadn't been a happy past seven months. The mood of the remaining staff was anything but uplifting. No one knew who would be next, and while most of the staff empathized with me, and my patients all assured me how much I'd be missed, it was time to move on.

I took the next month to look for similar positions. With nothing available in my own county or in the greater Orlando area, I applied for a Navigator position in one of the older hospitals in Volusia, the county just north of Brevard. In accepting it, however, I jumped feet first into another untenable situation. With no designated oncologist to administer the program (something which I hadn't been told), with one of the administrators who had hired me unexpectedly leaving for a better position in that organization, and with a manager who was neither a nurse nor in any way certified in oncology care, it was an absolute disaster.

I spent the next ten weeks commuting to that small hospital south of Daytona and east of Orlando, doing everything I could to stay busy. There were no new patient assignments, no direction, and no support from Radiation Oncology, which inexplicably directed the flow of patients. The Radiation Department secretary sent all patient-related calls to the social worker who, right away, saw my position there as a threat to hers, and the department manager did nothing to change it.

I spent ten weeks dutifully collecting data about patients newly diagnosed with cancer and wondering why I had been hired. Dejected and dealing with that hostile social worker and department secretary day after day, I made it through the holidays but knew something was up on the first day back after New Year's Day.

"We just don't see you as the right fit for us," the manager told me when she asked to speak with me after a department meeting.

I wanted to say, "As if anyone would have been the right fit!" Instead, I said, "And thank God for that!" and let her and her staff try to understand what I meant. This was another fight I'd gladly walk away from.

It was now 2011. Still not ready to retire, I admitted that my commitment to Oncology Advocacy and Patient Navigation had taken a pretty painful toll. I'd met some wonderful patients and families and had stretched and grown in a specialty that had been entirely new to me. Other options might have been available, but those were few, and the reality was that I had come full circle. Still both mentally and physically fit, I decided that if I wanted to make the best use of the years left to me, I would have to go back into hands-on patient care where I had started so many years before. The last thing I'd do is take a position with a physician who always put his wants and needs above those of his patients or with a program that had no clear direction and staff that did not accept or work with an Advocate and Navigator who did.

Chapter Twenty-Nine

ANOTHER NEW
LIFE BEGINS

GETTING BACK INTO hands-on care was much easier said than done.

Although not about to admit it to anyone, my ego had hit an all-time low. Experience and expertise gained in those many years in nursing should have counted for something, but, sadly, all the nursing positions I applied for required recent patient care experience. The last time I'd done actual hands-on patient care was in 2006.

In March, I interviewed for two positions that looked the most promising. The first was a Breast Cancer Navigator position at a hospital in Daytona, but, by now leery of working with another department manager in a program that also sent out negative vibes, I deferred a decision until after I interviewed for the second position. That was joining the staff of a new state-of-the-art facility closer to home, full-time night shifts with actual patients in a new post-surgical orthopedic unit.

The oncology position in Daytona didn't seem right for me, with a manager who reminded me of my old nemesis, Gisela Bach. I'd driven seventy miles to and from Orange City five days a week for ten weeks in that last regrettable position. I turned it down, accepted the second option, and commenced another adventure in nursing that tested me in more ways than I ever anticipated.

To say that I worried about taking on that new assignment would be a major understatement. I had always enjoyed direct patient care, but it had been a challenge during my long career to comfortably learn and utilize computerized medical records systems. Getting up to speed as quickly as possible in this new facility became my first priority. What terrified me was the current and rapidly evolving modern technology I needed to learn and utilize. Technology had always been a challenge for me.

More than thirty registered nurses, patient care techs, and unit coordinators had been hired to staff the Postoperative Orthopedic Surgical Unit in the new facility, and we all trained together to prepare for our new roles. Many of those thirty-plus already worked for the organization that hired us, but the rest of us struggled with the new electronic medical record system. With minimal need to access the electronic charting systems in my research and navigator positions the past four years, I was certain I would never learn this one.

As it turned out, in the fifteen months that I remained in that position, I did become skilled at electronic medical records and all the other technology required for patient care. I also loved the challenges in orthopedic nursing, which had been one of my favorites as a student nurse. It was the ways in which nursing and ancillary staff were treated in this new facility that became a problem.

This healthcare organization focused more on what staff members did wrong, telling us that "It's not the way we do it here" more often than "You did a great job with that patient." The unit manager, new to the role and determined to carry out the caveat of "Blame, don't praise," made working there increasingly hard to endure.

I had to admit that I didn't do my best work. I knew I had a lot to learn, but it soon became difficult just to report for each shift. Although senior to all the nurses in both education and experience, I was disrespected as well as challenged when the nursing that had always been my high standard of care differed from theirs. I was treated with courtesy and respect when I floated to other units, but the negativity and hostility of some colleagues in my own unit made working there almost unbearable. I was still working in a profession that I loved and had just celebrated the fiftieth anniversary of my graduation from Bellevue when it all came to a head in the summer of 2012.

Once I'd completed orientation to the new facility and become comfortable with the complicated computerized charting, I offered to work extra night shifts there and in the sister facility south of Melbourne. Because those shifts were awarded only to nurses favored by management, and because I could always benefit from more hands-on experience, I applied for and accepted a per diem position in a facility that cared for long-term, post-intensive care patients.

The shifts there were challenging, caring for extremely ill post-ICU patients. I learned yet another complicated electronic medical record charting system and how to use patient care equipment not seen before. I appreciated the courtesy of my new nursing colleagues, who welcomed the extra help staffing the units there and thanked me for providing those much-needed shifts.

Although I only worked there on my off-duty time, the nursing manager in my primary facility didn't approve. She called me one morning to schedule a meeting after I had completed another of them.

"Fine," I said. "What's it about?"

"We'll discuss it when you come in."

Three months before, she had called me in to discuss minor charting errors I'd made and the fact that I did not seem happy in the unit. "One of these days will be your decision day on whether you go or stay," she told me then.

Remembering that now, I said, "I worked last night and haven't slept, but I'll be happy to come in on Tuesday."

Anything but happy, annoyed that she wouldn't tell me the reason for the meeting, I knew it was time to take my life back.

She wasn't in her office when I arrived at the specified hour on Tuesday, and, for the second time in my professional life, I placed my name badge on a manager's desk and left a note: "This is my decision day."

I'd spent the past fifteen months trying to make an impossible position work, but I hadn't done my best work in that unit. I wished I could have done better, but I was grateful for what I had learned. I wasn't yet ready to give up on my career and was determined to make a success of my next position, wherever that happened to be.

Chapter Thirty

ADVENTURES IN TRAVEL NURSING

FOR THE REST of the summer, I continued per diem shifts at the long-term care facility and in a community hospital in Palm Coast, twenty miles north of Daytona. Then in September, I was offered a three-month travel nurse contract in a facility just ten miles from home. Another one was available in a community hospital across the state, but I would have been away from home for too long each week with far too much travel time back and forth to Merritt Island. Not sure I would even like the facility, I knew I needed more stability in my life after the stressful fifteen months in my first foray into patient care after oncology.

The three-month contract at that hospital close to home continued when I accepted a second contract. The work there was intense, three twelve-hour night shifts per week in medical units with challenging and complicated patients. I was amused when one of the oncology specialists with whom I'd worked as Advocate and Navigator saw me one night at work and gasped, "You're still doing bedside nursing?"

I laughed and said, "Well, yes, since it's always been the patients who have kept me in nursing." I meant it too. Despite the negativity of those colleagues in that prior hospital the year before, I admitted to myself that I would always be a work in progress. And I did learn in those next six months, adding to what I'd already learned, and looked forward to even more nursing challenges.

In March 2013, I accepted another travel assignment in a new facility in Daytona that I'd often driven past on the way to the hospital in Palm Coast. I'd hoped that someday I would be offered an assignment there and was delighted when it happened. The most recent sister hospital in the largest faith-based healthcare facility in Florida, it offered the opportunity I'd been looking for. The electronic medical record system was the one I used during those per diem shifts in the other facility in Palm Coast. I was impressed by the physical aspects of that new building, accessible to the I-95 freeway and an easy commute to Merritt Island. I would be there from March through June, working three to four 7 p.m. to 7 a.m. shifts each week and had no qualms about this latest contract. Those night shifts, with the frequent need to be on my feet and on the run for the entire shift, were a challenge I was happy to accept.

Most of my patients were elderly and suffering from many of the age-related comorbidities retirees lived with in addition to their primary diagnoses. At seventy-two, I was close to them in age, sharing similar life experiences. I was finally in my element, able to learn and do more in a positive and nurturing environment.

Like the rest of the staff, I floated to most other areas in the medical center and to the rehabilitation facility in Oceanside. The first time I reported in, I was hours behind medicating my patients and constantly forgetting passcodes into the medication room and equipment areas. I wasn't sure they would want me back, but I answered call lights, assisted the overworked patient care techs with demanding patients, and completed my own patient assignments in time for the change of shift reports to the oncoming staff. As I headed home that morning, the staff members on both shifts thanked me and invited me back.

The entire four months of that contract reinforced my resolve to keep working. Not all my goals had been met in a long and unconventional career, and I wasn't finished yet. When the contract ended, with declining patient censuses over the summer, I accepted per diem travel assignments north and south of Merritt Island. Quite often, shifts were canceled when regular staff members at those facilities became available to work, but the new contract stipulated that I would be paid if I committed to being available five shifts each week, even if I did not work. Not knowing until the last minute if I was actually working and having to travel at the last minute to wherever I'd been assigned made those summer months quite chaotic.

One memorable assignment in a small community hospital south of Melbourne was almost the end of me. It was the first time I had ever had no computer for charting. All the options I'd need would be on the cell phone the unit provided. Or so I thought. I'd had no orientation to the phone or how to carry out my charting that first night. I muddled through and went back hoping to do better, but this time two of the nurses, angry with each other about who was supposed to be in charge, refused to help.

A travel nurse who'd been there before got me through it, but I had such anxiety that my heart began to race—and kept right on racing. I knew what it was—a run of rapid atrial fibrillation—and I knew I didn't want to go down to Emergency to have it checked. That would have meant leaving all my patients for someone else to take over for the rest of the shift.

I did what I should NOT have done: I told no one, sat down quietly in the back of the room where we did documentation, and tried to calm down. After several long deep breaths, I was fine. My heart rate slowed down to normal, and I finished the shift, but I never went back to that facility and never told anyone why. Unfortunately, no new full-time contracts became available at the end of summer, and I finished out the year with that on-again, off-again schedule, including a temporary per diem assignment in a facility in New Smyrna Beach.

In January 2014, after my annual vacation in California and still not ready to retire, I didn't give up on finding a position that would, in due time, lead to the day when I would finally say, "That's it! I'm done!"

I was offered a travel assignment in Sebastian, at the southernmost end of Brevard County, and although it meant a great deal more driving down to Vero Beach and over to the Treasure Coast, I accepted it. I enjoyed the week-long orientation classes and the first week of patient care there, but the manager mandated an unworkable schedule—three nights on duty, one night off, then three more on—and refused to make any changes when I requested them. It would have meant more driving, more staying over at hotels in Sebastian County, and far less quality time off.

After one month, I left. The staff had been hostile as well, resenting all of us who were there temporarily, mistakenly believing that our salaries were higher than theirs. Not much had changed since registry shifts in California, except, in Florida, nurses still received far less pay than nurses in California and were almost always faced with impossibly problematic patient care assignments.

I went back to working per diem shifts again, hoping for a permanent contract that wouldn't be the end of me, and in February my recruiter called me with what I considered a miracle. She asked if I would accept a three-month assignment and a possible summer one in Daytona, in the facility where I'd been so happy the year before.

Chapter Thirty-One

BEGINNING AGAIN

I ACCEPTED THAT three-month assignment in Daytona, and at the end of the first week knew I wanted to be there on a permanent basis. The staff in the surgical unit remembered me and encouraged me to submit a full-time employment application that would coincide with the end of my travel contract.

I liked the unit and the patients and didn't mind floating to other units in the facility as well as to the Rehabilitation Center in Oceanside. Hoping for a permanent position at the end of my contract, I fulfilled my commitment to three shifts per week, occasionally worked a fourth, and was looking forward to the end of May when I received a telephone call from the Director of Personnel. "We're so sorry," she told me, "but we're going to rescind our offer of a full-time position. You failed to pass the physical examination as a condition of your employment."

I failed to pass?

I couldn't believe it. Everything had gone so well. I completed all the paperwork and knew that my travel nurse organization provided the required recommendations. The staff in the unit where I worked still approved. I'd been just a little surprised by the employment physical, somewhat more comprehensive than expected and taken two days prior, after a night shift at the Rehabilitation facility. Nothing about it had alarmed me at the time.

"You didn't lift a fifty-pound box and place it on a shelf over your head, and you didn't carry it the required distance," she told me. It was as if she were reading from a script. None of this lifting, placing, and carrying had been discussed before the exam, and no required standards had ever been explained, so all of this was news to me.

"You can't be serious!"

"Those are the rules, and we're sorry to have to enforce them," she said, ending the call. Still stunned, I thanked her for letting me know when I really felt more like screaming. I wished I had when I called the staffing coordinator a few minutes later to tell her about the canceled position and couldn't believe it when she said that I wouldn't be permitted to finish the remainder of my travel assignment.

"Because I didn't pass a physical exam that hadn't even been required when I accepted the contract? I was never told the requirements to pass the exam, had no time to prepare for it, and had just worked all night in the Oceanside facility. I never should have taken the exam at all! My blood pressure was 160/90 before I started, with no history of problems with hypertension. The person who tested me told me to go ahead with the physical anyway. I hate to think what it is right now!"

Fortunately, she recognized distress when she heard it and asked if I'd like to speak with the Administrator for Nursing.

"Yes, please. And as soon as possible!"

Fortunately, the Administrator for Nursing also recognized the problem and arranged for a second exam, one week later. I was determined to pass it this time and spent every day of the next week hefting a sixty-pound box of my favorite books up and down our long hallway at home, lifting it over my head and placing it on a shelf in the laundry room. Personnel's decision to rescind the job offer was placed on hold until after I'd taken the physical exam again, and, once again, I waited.

As hoped, I did pass it, better than expected. The contract was reinstated, and a $5,000 sign-on bonus was again offered.

Two years later, in the summer of 2016, I was still working, still meeting the goals set in 2014, still enjoying the challenge of patient care. The eighty-mile commute each way from Merritt Island to Daytona and back became a little easier with the I-95 reconstruction nearly completed, and I planned to work in nursing as long as my mind and body held up.

I used a portion of the sign-on bonus to take an advanced legal nurse course just in case I ever resumed Paper Chasers, then requested a change in status from full-time to part-time. It was time to get started on that personal history of my unconventional life in nursing. The idea for the book had been merely a glimmer after I ended my nursing role in oncology and returned to hands-on patient care. Nursing had been the defining role of my life. It had evolved into a long and unconventional career never envisioned at twenty. Actively working in my seventies and writing a book about it became my next challenge. In the summer of 2016, I finally started writing.

It took an entire year to complete the first draft, handwritten on yellow legal tablets. Still working two twelve-hour night shifts, I started the second draft during the day in the summer of 2017. Now typing the manuscript on my laptop and wondering if anyone would want to read it, I was thinking about making another change at work.

I enjoyed those Monday and Saturday night shifts, learned as much as I'd hoped to learn with our post-operative surgical patients but still needed more nursing challenges to keep my skills current. Because I frequently floated to the Surgical Progressive Care Unit and found the staff to be appreciative and supportive, I began to consider making the change. When one of my colleagues there recommended me to the manager that November, I decided to apply for a part-time position transfer.

With one delay after another, it took until mid-December to make it official, but, first, I had to accomplish three things: improve my deplorable medication scanning technique, apply for and pass the next available Advanced Cardiac Life Support class, and apply for and accept the new transfer to the Surgical Progressive Care Unit. The last one should have been the easiest to accomplish, but I learned almost too late that it was an offer for a newly created position, not a transfer, and I almost missed the deadline to call the recruiter with my acceptance.

Medication scanning should have been simple as well, but, at the time, I was the absolute worst at scanning patients' wristbands in order to provide their medications. I had just about given up ever getting past that fifty percent success rate when my soon-to-be new manager set me up with the computer system guru in the facility's education office.

Malfunctioning scanners and handheld computers had been a major part of the problem, but my new best friend in computer education focused immediately on my issues with the process. I hadn't always found the exact spot on the patient wristband when I scanned it. That issue disappeared when she corrected my scanning technique. I improved from that deplorable fifty percent to well over a consistent ninety-five percent, good enough to meet the second requirement for my new position.

The second, passing the next available Advanced Cardiac Life Support class, was the most perplexing of the three. I'd already purchased and begun to study the most recent ACLS manual but ran up against a major obstacle when attempting to register for the first available class at my own facility in January. That class was already filled. "Take your chances, show up, and maybe there will be a place for you," the instructor told me. I knew that wasn't good enough.

The recruiter also confirmed it. "I'll keep the position open until January 7th," she told me. "You'll have to take ACLS somewhere else and not start in Surgical Progressive Care until you've passed it."

No new classes in our sister hospitals had been scheduled until February, so I opted for the training facility in one of the county's other major healthcare organizations. It required a $150 fee, which my own facility would not reimburse, as well as a drive down to the training center in Melbourne, but I did it gladly, determined to meet that most important obligation.

I studied ACLS and all the scenarios needed to pass the course—and the dreaded Mega Code—until I felt comfortable enough to take the self-assessment required for the January class. Past and present nursing managers had agreed I could begin working in the unit before taking and passing the course. I would be assigned solely to post-surgical patients, the same type of patients I cared for when floated to that unit.

The January class wasn't my first. Counting early ACLS courses in the 1960s and later ones in the 1970s, 1980s, 1990s, and 2000s, I'd taken the course at least fifteen times so was not especially concerned about this one.

The first day of class was fine, with two experienced healthcare professionals who thrived at what they did for a living and made the extensive review of systems and scenarios almost enjoyable. The second day was another story. Devoted entirely to the Mega Code, it was even tougher than some of those earlier courses in California. This instructor, a retired registered nurse in her sixties, was hard on all of us, but she focused most of her criticism on me.

Determined to survive her, I tolerated every negative remark, went through four additional turns at the monitor/defibrillator until perfect, and braced for the final turn as Code Team Leader. My transfer to the Progressive Care Unit depended on passing that Mega Code, even if it almost killed me. My fellow classmates were as surprised as I was at how merciless she was. Nothing I did satisfied her. Although I successfully completed all the scenarios, she made it seem almost pointless to continue. I needed that certification, so I soldiered on until she finally admitted that I knew all the sequences as well as she did.

That afternoon, I aced the written exam and left the training center happy to have put the ACLS ordeal behind me. As I handed in my exam, the instructor apologized for having been so rough on me. "You did fine. You knew every one of those scenarios. I just wanted to be absolutely certain you would be ready to transfer into Progressive Care."

"Thanks," I said, now that I'd survived it. "But I thought the point of this class was to prepare us to participate in actual Code Blues. I had participated in dozens of Codes before you made today such an ordeal. If your intent was to make us dread taking another class like this one, you succeeded."

I reported to Surgical Progressive Care the next night. Because I'd worked there before and knew the layout of the unit, I simply needed updates on charting specific to SPCU and on medication and monitoring protocols for surgical with patients with cardiac comorbidities. And I did learn. Those patients were similar to the ones I cared for in the Post-Surgical Unit for the past three-and-a-half years, but most had many more problems than simply post-operative surgical care. In my former unit, no one was admitted with an infection and anyone who was even possibly infected was transferred, usually to SPCU. There, many of the patients were placed in isolation for a variety of reasons, which meant incorporating isolation procedures for those patients as well as safe nursing practice for all those other non-infected patients.

Now, frequently, two of the five assigned to me required isolation, but occasionally there was a third one in standard isolation, on droplet precautions, or in neutropenic precautions post-chemotherapy. That made those twelve-hour night shifts a great deal more stressful, but I had taken the position in Surgical Progressive Care to prove to myself I could still do it, so the tougher the shift, the better.

Nursing colleagues on day and night shifts respected me for working past the age when most nurses did, for often racing around the unit faster than they did, and for still answering call lights and providing compassionate hands-on care to my patients. Those patients, often my age or older, felt comfortable having someone of their generation able to communicate with them on their level, to share life stories, and to see them through their tragedies and triumphs.

I was still very much a work in progress. Not everything was smooth or easy, and I often left for home in the mornings wishing I'd provided better patient care, had given better shift-to-shift reports, and done more to make the next few hours easier for the oncoming staff. But I kept right on trying.

In April, just after turning seventy-seven, I came up against a problem that would have made simply driving to work impossible. Required to provide documentation to renew my driver's license in person, I was told that my birth certificate, issued in Boston, wasn't official since it didn't provide a first or middle name, just "female" and my last name.

Because of all the heightened scrutiny on documentation since 9/11, that birth certificate, as well as the one from the state of Massachusetts (also with no first or middle name), were not accepted. With both parents deceased, and no one alive after all those years to correctly identify me, I couldn't renew the driver's license, couldn't commute to Daytona, and couldn't drive anywhere else. Some problem or other always seemed to be waiting to complicate my life. Taking away my right to drive was the last straw. "What do I do now?" I asked the clerk.

Fortunately, this one at the Brevard County Department of Motor Vehicles had a heart and understood the problem. "What else do you have?" she asked, indicating the file folder I'd brought with me containing all the documents that should have been sufficient. When I showed her the two Army Nurse Corps commissions, the original one in 1963 and the subsequent one in 1989, she used them to have those insufficient birth certificates grandfathered in. If the Army had accepted me twice with no name, so could the state of Florida!

I was so grateful that I went home and wrote her a personal thank you for her kindness. A week or so later, I was surprised when I received a thank you letter of my own, not from her but from her superior, the Brevard County Tax Assessor.

"Thank you for your kind letter to my colleague at the Department of Motor Vehicles. It is thoughtful and most appreciated. No one has ever taken the time before now to compliment the members of my staff on their service."

And I had never before received such a warm and thoughtful response!

Chapter Thirty-Two

A SPLENDID GIFT

AS AUGUST CAME to an end, I continued the long drive to Daytona twice a week, determined to provide the best possible care to my patients. In my fifty-seventh year since graduation and sixtieth since starting as a student at Bellevue, I was grateful for the career chosen so many years ago. I wouldn't have traded those challenging, exhausting, and frequently frustrating sixty years for anything. And as always, when colleagues and friends asked when I planned to retire, I would simply say, "Not yet."

Not everything about those years had been easy, and far too often I had taken one step forward and two steps back. I accepted but had never embraced all the recent technology that put such a distance between us and our patients, and lately I asked myself, *What is management thinking when they insist that we carry a telephone and walkie-talkie 'for better patient safety'?*

I asked one of my coworkers the same thing the first time I heard about it.

"You've got that right," she said. "What are we supposed to do if we're in an Isolation room or trying to stop a patient from falling out of bed? Forget about it and answer those damned things? Both of them?"

It would have been better if our nurse leaders provided the support

we needed to safely care for our growing numbers of mentally or neurologically challenged patients. It would have been far better if they
spent more time and energy on staff satisfaction that would prevent so
many of us from transferring out of our units or from leaving nursing
entirely.

As summer ended and I had almost completed my first year in
Surgical Progressive Care, it became harder and harder to accept those
trying twelve-hour shifts. With declining patient care technician support and decreasing support from management to address our most
pressing issues, unrest ran high in Surgical Progressive Care, and no
one seemed at all happy to be there.

Some staff members felt comfortable only in the nurses' station,
commiserating with each other, endlessly texting or calling friends or
family on their cell phones, and not being anywhere near the rooms
where their patients needed closer monitoring. Not every shift began
or ended badly, and most of the time I welcomed the challenges, but I
often needed an entire day after each shift to fully recover.

Driving to work in Daytona wasn't a problem unless it was rain-
ing. A hazard at any time due to reckless drivers and endless freeway
reconstruction, heavy rains over I-95 often made it impossible to see
anything in front of me, beside me, or behind me. Even more harrow-
ing was driving eighty miles home after twelve-hour shifts that turned
into thirteen or fourteen. That often meant pulling off the freeway at
44 East, a junction for New Smyrna Beach, and snatching a quick nap
in my car in the parking lot at Walmart. Driving any farther than that
was just an invitation to disaster. I know it bothered my daughters,
who never stopped worrying about me. "You're over seventy, Mom!"
they reminded me. "You shouldn't even be working, and especially not
doing all that driving!"

What made work more trying was the departure of several dedicated staff nurses and techs and the unexpected resignation of the
nurse manager who, for me, had always been understanding and supportive. She encouraged and patiently supported me through my trials

with missing computers and malfunctioning scanners, and after read-ing the first three chapters of the book she knew I was writing, she sent me a note that I will always treasure. "You are amazing!" she wrote. "I love that you embrace nursing and have such a rich history with this honorable profession!"

After she resigned, I considered moving to the new Rehabilitation Unit on our facility's twelfth floor, the replacement for the Oceanside building that had been too badly damaged in the last hurricane to undergo renovation. That move would have been another challenge to meet before I finally retired, but I was still determined to fulfill those commitments I'd made to my prior manager when she hired me, so I decided to tough it out in the Surgical Progressive Care Unit.

My husband and I took a trip north to New York and Connecticut in October to visit both our East Coast families, and, in November, he finally underwent his long-postponed right total knee replacement. The recovery from this surgery was more stressful for him than the first one eight years before. At seventy-eight, he was not enjoying this most recent setback since his 2003 retirement, and we both agreed that getting older wasn't for sissies!

He had just begun to finally recover from that surgery and gone back to his favorite pastime, bowling, when he had the heart attack that took his life. For dying hearts, time is muscle, and the sooner in-dividuals with chest pain or discomfort that doesn't seem normal are examined and treated, the better their chance for survival.

"I'm fine!" he insisted that Thursday night after bowling. "It's just my shoulder. I must have strained it." He never admitted how bad it was, and his heart began to fail that night when he experienced what he later told his physician was "the worst pain I've ever had."

Always stubborn about seeking medical care and refusing to ac-cept it when it was provided, he never acknowledged that I actually knew a thing or two about healthcare. He refused to see his physician or go to the Emergency Department that night or the next day or the next. When he finally went to see his physician on the fourth day, it was too late. The damage had been catastrophic.

His right heart started to fail, and he now experienced one of the worst possible cardiac complications, a VSR, ventricular septal rupture of the wall separating the right heart from the left. His cardiologists at the hospital where he underwent two procedures to unblock and stent the right coronary artery meticulously tracked his cardiac function and diagnosed the rupture on his fifth hospital day. They contacted the team of cardiovascular surgeons at the Heart Institute and sent him by Life Flight to Melbourne for the surgery they hoped would save his life.

Cranky and cantankerous as he now so often was, my husband was thrilled with the flight, and as the medics wheeled him out of ICU on the way to the Helipad, he waved to all of us and called out, "Adios, good people!"

More than ten hours in open-heart surgery and an extremely rocky recovery kept him alive, but chances were slim to none that he would ever recover cardiac function on his own. He had asked his surgeons to do everything possible to save him, but they had known, as I had, that it wouldn't be possible. On the fourteenth day after the initial heart attack, I made the painful decision to discontinue life support.

His long ordeal brought our blended families closer in love and support, and because he survived far longer than they had anticipated, the surgical and critical care staffs learned valuable lessons on how to treat and save the next patient with such a deadly and final diagnosis.

Because of my extensive career in nursing and experiences with critically ill patients, I was an added source of strength and support for family and friends, none of whom had any experience in critical care and couldn't fully understand what was happening that long and heartbreaking six days after John's surgery. We somehow got through it, with sadness and regret and certain knowledge that our lives without him would change forever. The thirty-nine years he and I shared had passed so quickly, and so much had been left unsaid. I did tell him, awake and still able to hear me before he left for surgery, "I love you, and I'll see you later." But we both knew that these words would probably be our last words together.

And now the time had come to make some decisions of my own.

My husband and daughters never liked my long drives back and forth to work in Daytona. I had been thinking about retiring in June but now had a household to maintain alone and goals of my own still to be met, so, the week after John died, I made that last drive to Daytona to announce my decision to retire. It was time to say good-bye.

And, yes, I was a little tearful. This end of my life in nursing was not at all like the beginning at Bellevue. This last job, staff nurse in Surgical Progressive Care, was nothing like my first job as a Charge Nurse on D-3. Those days as a brand-new nurse, learning my craft in one of the most famous medical centers in the country, would remain forever in my memory. They prepared me well for all the challenges to come, challenges I so often feared would overwhelm me in the many years since Bellevue, where, somehow, I had met them all.

As I looked down that long, well-lighted hallway in the medical center I was leaving, I couldn't help comparing it to the dim, dark hallways in that centuries-old hospital where I began my long, ex-traordinary career. So much had changed in all those years since I left Bellevue. This medical center, which so beautifully addressed the spir-itual as well the physical well-being of its patients and staff had every modern convenience. Each patient had a single room. Everything was done to ensure that the best possible care was provided; the patients had their families with them for as long and as often as they wanted them, and no request was ignored.

In this last professional nursing assignment, I had no more than five patients each shift, all the necessary equipment and support I needed, and far better staffing than I'd ever had at Bellevue. But some things had been the same. I was still on the run the entire shift, still wishing for more time to complete every task. I was still keeping vigil over the most vulnerable patients, still providing endless medications on time, and still trying to stay ahead of the constant requests for pain relief. Above all, I was still doing whatever could be done for each patient who, for me, always had a name and not just a room number.

I left for home after each shift, just as I had done at Bellevue, wishing I could have done better during those long hours on duty and always grateful when things went well. So, yes, I was just a little tearful as I said my last goodbye.

Nursing gave my life dedication and purpose, and I made a difference in the lives of multitudes of patients and their families. More than six decades after Sister Marie Cecilia saw potential in that awkward, unformed fifteen-year-old, I think she would have been proud of the woman I had become, and I know she would have agreed that my long and extraordinary life in nursing had indeed been a splendid gift.

EPILOGUE

ON MARCH 15, 2020, my sister Carroll turned eighty and I turned seventy-nine. That same week, everyone in this country became painfully aware that the COVID-19 pandemic that had already devastated China and had taken hold in Italy was about to overwhelm us. Both Carroll and I were registered nurses, retired after long and fulfilling careers, but neither of us had ever had to face a healthcare crisis as dire as this one. Because of our ages, we'd be among the most vulnerable to contract the disease, so returning to work to take care of patients was not an option.

My heart went out to all my colleagues in healthcare who now faced a deadly disease that would take so many millions of lives. While we had to stay home and shelter in place, they and everyone in this country who supported their efforts had no choice but to risk their lives and report to work to do whatever they could to save their patients.

As I write this in December, they are still out there, still putting their lives at risk as the latest deadly wave of COVID-19 rages on. I commend all of them, my sisters and brothers in nursing, all the physicians, the first responders, and support personnel who battle this invisible and invincible enemy. Their commitment has been and continues to be their splendid gift to us.

December 24, 2020

POSTSCRIPT

IN 2021, THREE years after I retired, I learned firsthand how it felt to be a patient facing a real-life healthcare crisis. During my six decades in nursing, I had helped countless patients endure similar circumstances. Now it was my turn to face loss of control, loss of dignity, and possible loss of life.

After a weekend of exhaustion, abdominal pain, and a cough, which I convinced myself was just the flu, I took two COVID tests, both negative, and made an appointment to see my physician. Something was wrong. I could barely take two steps without shortness of breath, and thought of my dear sister Carroll, who had died in April of a rare type of pneumonia. It never occurred to me that it could be my heart.

The Nurse Practitioner at my physician's office immediately diagnosed uncontrolled atrial fibrillation with rapid ventricular response. My heart rate was 160 and my blood pressure an alarming 180/100. She sent me to the closest medical facility, and although I walked into Emergency on my own two feet, I was triaged at once and whisked back to one of the treatment rooms for an IV, lab work, and a second EKG. It was uncontrolled atrial fib. I also had congestive heart failure and was in imminent danger of a stroke. There was no way I would go home that day.

I spent ten hours in Emergency receiving anti-arrhythmia

medication, antihypertensives, and anticoagulants to prevent that massive stroke. None of the medications reversed the fibrillation, so I was admitted to the Cardiac Unit, where I finally came to terms with the fact that I could die.

I spent four full days and nights at Rockledge Regional Medical Center. My children were all on the West Coast, in California and Washington. I texted them not to worry and not to race to still pandemic-ravaged Florida. My dear companion, Joe, stood in for them. We'd been bowling friends for years, and now, both widowed, were in a committed relationship. He was by my side the entire time I was in the hospital.

A trans-esophageal echocardiogram revealed an otherwise healthy heart with no clots, well-functioning valves, and a suspected electrical conduction problem in my right atrium. Four cardioversions only temporarily overrode the fibrillation, and I relied on intravenous and oral medications to treat it and the congestive heart failure.

I went home the evening of my fourth full day at the medical center. My comrades in healthcare had saved me, with competence and compassion. Patient care technology had come a long way since my student days at Bellevue, and I probably wouldn't have survived as well, or at all, if my accelerating and stubborn atrial fibrillation had occurred then. After four weeks of recuperation at home, with heart rate and blood pressure returning to normal, I sent a letter to the CEO of the medical center where I'd been a patient.

"Not enough people will say 'thank you' in these troubling times," I wrote. "But I do thank you and the entire healthcare team who cared for me during my incredible and most memorable hospital experience." And I meant every word of it.

In December, Amiodarone caused a toxic reaction, I was in congestive heart failure, and both lungs had begun filling with fluid. Physicians hadn't expected bilateral pleural effusions, but aggressive diuretics resolved that problem, and this time cardioversion resolved the atrial flutter. The same competent and compassionate nursing and technical staff welcomed me back, I had another four days of excellent care, and I went home after surviving another healthcare crisis.

Three months later, atrial fibrillation and flutter have not returned, cardiac catheterization and angiography reveal no coronary occlusions and no damage to my heart muscle. All my medications are effective. I have retuned to my normal, active life. Increasing nursing expertise and evolving biomedical technology have saved me twice, and I am grateful for the opportunity to complete this memoir.

March 2022

www.ingramcontent.com/pod-product-compliance
Lightning Source LLC
Chambersburg PA
CBHW041718090426
42739CB00018B/3464